U-BOAT COMMAND AND THE BATTLE OF THE ATLANTIC

U-BOAT COMMAND
AND
THE BATTLE OF THE ATLANTIC

by

Jak Mallmann Showell

219663

CONWAY
MARITIME PRESS

First published in Great Britain in 1989 by
Conway Maritime Press Ltd
24 Bride Lane, Fleet Street
London EC4Y 8DR

British Library Cataloguing in Publication Data

Showell, Jak P. Mallmann (Jak Peter Mallmann),
  1944–
  U. Boat Command and the battle of the
  Atlantic
  1. World War 2. North Atlantic Campaign.
  Naval operations by Germany, Kriegsmarine.
  Submarines
  I. Title
  940.54′21

  ISBN 0–85177–487–3

Designed by Roger Lightfoot
Typeset by Inforum Ltd, Portsmouth
Printed and Bound by Richard Clay Ltd, Bungay

Contents

Acknowledgements and Unpublished Sources

In 1976, this project was abandoned after three years of research. Though Grand Admiral Karl Dönitz lent me private papers and gave me permission to consult his war diary, at a time when it was still a restricted document, I discovered that for every question answered many more emerged and it seemed as if the study was taking me further away from the goal.

During the summer of 1976, while passing through Munich, Kpt.z.S. a.D. Otto Köhler asked me to reconsider this decision. Kpt.z.S. a.D. Ajax Bleichrodt put it a little more forcefully, saying, 'There can be no question of you abandoning the Dönitz project. Political sensitivity prevents Germans from writing their own history and foreigners do not understand our navy. So you have got to do it'. Otto and Ajax must be thanked because this project would never have been completed without their encouragement.

Great care has been taken to avoid relying on people's memories. Konteradmiral a.D. Eberhard Godt (ex-head of the U-boat Command) summed up the problems by saying, 'With some things I cannot remember whether I experienced them, whether someone told me, whether I read the information or whether it was a dream'. I have also tried to avoid postwar documents and based the majority of this book on evidence recorded before 1947. A great deal of the material in the book is based on the following unpublished sources and it is from these that the quotations in the book are taken.

— The U-boat Command's War Diary (Kriegstagebuch des Führer der Unterseeboote and Befehlshaber der Unterseeboote. Both these positions were held by Karl Dönitz, but much of the diary was compiled by Eberhard Godt, who was the Chief of the Operations Department which later became known as U-boat Command).

— The U-boat Command's Card Index of U-boats (Ubootskartei).

— The War Diary of the Supreme Naval Command (KTB der 1. SKL, Teil B, Heft IV, Ubootskrieg).

— Reports from Flotilla Commanders and from U-boat Flag Officers.

— Logs from individual U-boats.

— The Secret Diary of Oberfunkmeister Wolfgang Hirschfeld. (This has now been published. See Select Bibliography.)

– British anti-submarine reports.
– A three volume monograph of the U-boat War, compiled immediately after the war by two distinguished U-boat commanders and U-boat Command Staff Officers, Kpt.z.S. Günter Hessler and Kpt.z.S. Alfred Hoschatt. They compiled this monograph for the Royal Navy and it can be taken as Germany's only 'official history' of the U-boat war.

In addition to these records, I have consulted other documents at the German U-boat Archive, the Royal Navy's Submarine Museum at HMS *Dolphin*, the United States National Archives and Records Administration and the Bundesarchiv. I am especially grateful to Horst Bredow, Commander Richard Compton-Hall and Gus Britton for making my visits possible and for guiding me through their extensive records. I should also like to thank Dr Timothy Mulligan for his help.

During the fifteen years of research my wife and I travelled thousands of miles through Europe to visit many people who have helped me understand the incidents recorded in log books. The majority of these helpers have been listed in the two books which I wrote while researching this one and I hope that a general word of thanks will be accepted here. Above all, I hope that this book will repay my dept by presenting an honest account of the U-boat Command's Battle in the Atlantic.

Photographs have kindly been supplied by: The German U-boat Archive, RN Submarine Museum at HMS *Dolphin*, Ajax Bleichrodt, Heinrich Böhm, Gus Britton, Ernst-August Gerke, Otto Giese, Wolfgang Hirschfeld, Karl Keller, Otto Köhler, Hermann Patzke, Paul Preuss, Edward Rumpf, Franz Selinger, Knut Sivertsen (Trondheim Defence Museum), Kath Showell, Paul Popper and the author's collection.

Introduction

The Anglo-German Naval Agreement of 1935 brought about considerable administrative problems by permitting far more submarines than had been anticipated to be re-introduced into the German Navy. Plans to attach the few which were expected to be permitted to torpedo boat or destroyer flotillas had to be scrapped and plans made to create an autonomous U-boat unit. The appointment of a suitable leader for this unit posed a considerable problem. Submariners from World War I had either retired or risen beyond the rank usually held by a small flotilla commander and the new blood, being trained secretly under the guise of an anti-submarine school, was not yet mature enough to hold such exacting office. At this critical stage, just as the vacuum in the leadership was starting to create problems, the light cruiser *Emden* returned from a world cruise. Her 44-year-old commander, with 25 years of service, Fregattenkapitän Karl Dönitz, was just the person to be temporarily shunted into the awkward position of Submarine Flotilla Commander. His 30 months of submarine experience during the last phase of the Great War was of minor importance when considering his other attributes. He had commissioned two brand new units: first, a torpedo boat half flotilla and second, following a lengthy refit, he had brought the light cruiser *Emden* back into service with a new crew. In addition to this, he had shown himself to be a brilliant leader with considerable vision, who was able to work on his own without having to follow the rule book.

In the end, Dönitz's temporary appointment lasted for four years and the war started before his successor, Hans-Georg von Friedeburg, could take over. Faced with conflict at sea, it was thought best for Dönitz to continue with operational matters and for von Friedeburg to take on the more complicated Organisation Department. The administrative pattern had created these two major sub-divisions within the small U-boat force. The Organisation Department was responsible for getting boats ready for action, but once at sea boats from all the flotillas came under the jurisdiction of an operations department. By the end of the first week of war, this operations department was run by Kapitän zur See und Kommodore Karl Dönitz, supported by his First Staff Officer, Korvetten-Kapitän Eberhard Godt. The small operations department grew in

Konteradmiral Eberhard Godt joined the navy at the end of World War I; after 1935 he served briefly as U-boat commander and in 1939 became head of the U-boats' operations department. His character contrasted greatly with that of Dönitz, and he was once described as 'a brilliant and modest Prussian gentleman, whom one would associate more with a professor of the arts rather than aggressive fighting leader'. Throughout the war he was responsible for the routine running of the U-boat Command.

The author was one of the few researchers who had Grand Admiral Karl Dönitz's permission to consult the U-boat Command's war diary at a time when it was still classified as secret in both Great Britain and the United States.

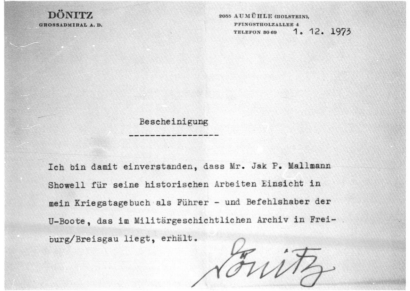

importance to become one of the most significant sub-divisions of the Naval War Staff. To U-boat men, it became known simply as the U-boat Command.

This book tries to follow the Battle of the Atlantic through the eyes and experiences of this small operations department which became The U-boat Command. The titles of its two main leaders as well as the official name of the department were changed as they grew in importance, but I have tried to restrict myself to using the same general terms throughout the book.

It is difficult to compile a comprehensive account of the whole of the Battle of the Atlantic in a single volume and in this book I have concentrated on how the U-boat Command perceived the Battle of the Atlantic; on the actions which they took and the reasons behind their decisions. Present day views of the Battle of the Atlantic were formulated shortly after the war while details of many events were still obscured by battle smoke and before statistics could be compiled for a detailed analysis. Since then, most authors have simply retold the same story. The following outline, which is somewhat different from the conventional view, is intended to give an idea of the basic pattern of the war.

It is envisaged that many readers will select a few chapters for study rather than go through the book from beginning to end. Therefore, a number of points have been mentioned more than once. I hope that readers who do read the book from end to end will be patient with the various points of repetition.

The Approach to Unrestricted Sea Warfare: September 1939–March 1940

Hitler's orders curtailing naval action, shortly after Britain and France declared war, resulted in a period of relative inactivity for U-boats. Being tied by Prize Ordinance Regulations and lacking definite instructions, the U-boat Command tried to obtain clarification of orders and, at the same time, a lifting of the seemingly impossible limitations. From October onwards, the restrictions were slowly eased, but their total abolition, leading to a state of unrestricted sea warfare did not come about until August 1940.

As the war progressed, the preoccupations of the U-boat Command shifted from action at sea to mechanical problems at home. Faults which developed both in the boats and in the torpedoes came to a head during the Norwegian Campaign of April 1940 when the German Navy suffered catastrophic torpedo failures. Mines, especially the magnetic variety, became an important weapon during the first winter of the war. Naval operations came to an abrupt halt in March 1940 when all forces were directed to participate in the invasion of Norway.

The Happy Time: May–November 1940

The numerous torpedo failures of the Norwegian Campaign led Dönitz to think that he might have to face a rebellion and he was most apprehensive in May when U-boats returned to the North Atlantic. Air waves were initially dominated by reports of more failures, but these gave way to successes which marked the beginning of the most successful period of the whole war. The havoc caused by the small number of U-boats was due mainly to surface attack at night. U-boats were used as torpedo boats, attacking during the hours of darkness when tall merchant ships stood out against the lighter sky, while the thin silhouettes of U-boats could hardly be seen. For much of this time boats operated on their own. Occasionally, several were called together for a group attack, but the famous wolf pack technique, where patrol lines were formed to find convoys, did not feature until 1941. Worsening winter weather eventually helped to bring a respite in U-boat activities.

The Collapse of the U-Boat Offensive: February–November 1941

Statistics showing the collapse of the U-boat offensive during 1941 are supported by comments in the U-boat Command's war diary, but at the time this lack of success was taken as a temporary

Admiral Hans-Georg von Friedeburg was due to have followed Dönitz as Flag Officer for Submarines, but the war started too soon and he took on the much more complex Organisation Department instead. A year before the end of the war, he told his wife that he would not accept the humiliation of being taken a prisoner-of-war and shortly after his arrest at the end of the war von Friedeburg kept his word and committed suicide.

setback. The collapse started around the time when U47 (KL Günter Prien), U70 (KL Joachim Matz), U99 (KL Otto Kretschmer) and U100 (KL Joachim Schepke) were sunk. From then on, U-boats had to work harder to find targets, attacking became more difficult and 1941 ended with disasterous losses. The battle for Convoy HX76 and the sinking of the escort carrier *Audacity* were important elements in this decline. The British managed to route merchant shipping around patrol lines because they were able to decipher large proportions of the German radio code, but the Royal Navy did not yet have sufficient resources to hunt U-boats to extinction. Although many convoy routes were identified by the B-Dienst (Radio Monitoring Service), U-boats experienced considerable difficulties in finding their targets and 1941 saw the evolution of the wolf pack techniques. Activities in the North Atlantic came to a halt in November when the Supreme Naval Command ordered boats to be moved to Gibraltar, where they concentrated on disrupting the British supply routes to North Africa.

Operations in American Waters: January–May 1942

This period, which has often been described as the Second Happy or Second Golden Time, was somewhat out of character. The large number of ships sunk was not a result of German ingenuity, but due almost entirely to American negligence. Continuing to sail her traffic as in peacetime, the United States failed to take any significant countermeasures and war-hardened U-boats found it easy to sink the virtually defenceless ships. For any statistical analysis, therefore, it should be remembered that few of the ships would have gone down if America had adopted techniques already used by Britain.

Return to Mid-Atlantic: May 1942–March 1943

The successes along the eastern seaboard of the United States belied many problems and worries at U-boat Command. These increased once U-boats made another effort to regain a foothold in the convoy routes of the North Atlantic. Increased submarine construction, ordered as late as the summer of 1940, started to make an impact and the ever increasing numbers of U-boats paved the way for the biggest convoy battle of the war. Although this period has often been regarded as the climax of the U-boat offensive, the performance of individual U-boats had steadily declined. The largest convoy battle of the war took place in March 1943, after the Germans had had a hundred U-boats at sea each day for six months.

In March, 40 ships of the fast convoy HX229 caught up with the 50-strong slow convoy SC122, just as one of the biggest wolf packs was closing around them. The subsequent carnage was partly due to mechanical failures on the allied side, an Enigma blackout in London and unfortunate circumstances which left room for a number of inexperienced U-boat commanders to launch torpedoes.

The End of the Wolf Packs: May 1943–March 1944

Claims that May 1943 saw the collapse of the U-boat offensive can be supported neither by statistics, nor by historical documents. A large number of U-boats were sunk but the month did not witness any other significant changes. The new equipment, such as detection devices and the weapons used to sink U-boats, had been available for some time. What had changed was that the Royal Navy now had sufficient ships to start hunting U-boats more rigorously. Dönitz did not perceive May as having been the turning point of the war and, indeed, he maintained until the very end of the war that U-boats remained unchallenged as primary weapons. The summer of 1943 saw the gradual introduction by the Germans of new equipment such as better radar detectors, more powerful anti-aircraft guns and new torpedoes, but none of these had much impact on the disastrous situation at sea. Only in February 1944 did Dönitz finally admit that the Atlantic was no longer a viable

Dönitz, as Vizeadmiral, greeting the crew of U96. From left to right: Obermaate Geissler and Friedrich, and Materosengefreite Katter and Pitschnik. Note the rank insignia on the lapels.

*Supreme Naval
Command
Departments at the
start of the war*

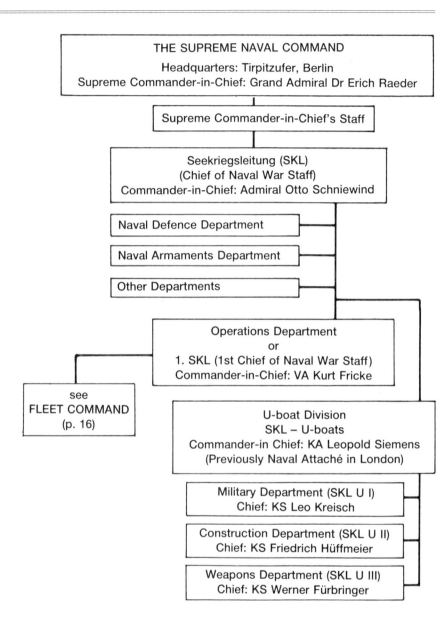

THE SUPREME NAVAL COMMAND

Headquarters: Tirpitzufer, Berlin
Supreme Commander-in-Chief: Grand Admiral Dr Erich Raeder

Supreme Commander-in-Chief's Staff

Seekriegsleitung (SKL)
(Chief of Naval War Staff)
Commander-in-Chief: Admiral Otto Schniewind

Naval Defence Department

Naval Armaments Department

Other Departments

Operations Department
or
1. SKL (1st Chief of Naval War Staff)
Commander-in-Chief: VA Kurt Fricke

see
FLEET COMMAND
(p. 16)

U-boat Division
SKL – U-boats
Commander-in Chief: KA Leopold Siemens
(Previously Naval Attaché in London)

Military Department (SKL U I)
Chief: KS Leo Kreisch

Construction Department (SKL U II)
Chief: KS Friedrich Hüffmeier

Weapons Department (SKL U III)
Chief: KS Werner Fürbringer

proposition for U-boat activity and it was then that the convoy war virtually came to a halt. After that date operations were concentrated in remoter regions.

The Allied Invasion of Europe and the End of the Battle of the Atlantic: June 1944–May 1945

Following the allied invasion of Europe, U-boats evacuated their French Atlantic bases to re-group in Norway. Small scale operations continued, especially in coastal waters, but Dönitz turned his attention to the Baltic where the German Navy was making a desperate effort to help evacuate millions of Germans from the path of the advancing Russian armies.

RANKS

In writing this book I have used the authentic German terms. The majority of these are followed by a translation, but the use of German ranks might not be so easy to follow. They were:

Commander-in-Chief U-boats: Karl Dönitz.

Grossadmiral: Admiral of the Fleet
Generaladmiral: Not used in Britain
Admiral: Admiral
Vizeadmiral (VA): Vice Admiral
Konteradmiral (KA): Rear Admiral
Kommodore: Commodore (Captain in a
    post usually held by an admiral) .
Kapitän zur See (KS): Captain
Fregattenkapitän (FK): Captain (Junior)
Korvettenkapitän (KK): Commander
Kapitänleutnant (KL): Lieutenant-
    Commander
Oberleutnant zur See (OL): Lieutenant
    (Senior)
Leutnant zur See (LS): Lieutenant (Junior)
Oberfähnrich zur See: Sub-Lieutenant
Fähnrich zur See: Midshipman/Cadett
Oberbootsmann[1]: Chief Boatswain
Bootsmann[1]: Boatswain
Ober--maat[2]: Chief Petty Officer
--maat[2] : Petty Officer
Matrose: Ordinary Seaman

Notes
1. If the man had a special occupation, his trade would have been

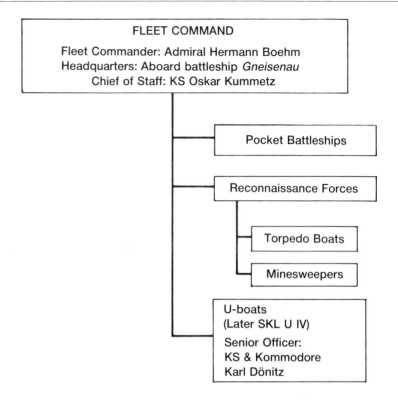

used instead of the word 'boot'. Eg Maschinist, Funkmeister etc.
2. The man's trade would have been used in place of the two
hyphens. Eg Funkmaat, Torpedomaat.

Further information about positions held within the U-boat
Command, organisation of the U-boat arm and mechanical details
of boats can be found in my earlier books *U-boats under the
Swastika* and *The German Navy in World War Two*. See bibliography.

1. Overtures of War

Karl Dönitz ranks as one of the most misunderstood men of World War II. There has been a widespread tendency to over-estimate his prewar powers and, after he was promoted to Supreme Commander-in-Chief of the Navy, to reproach him for not having acted like a rebellious junior officer. At the start of the war, he was at the bottom of a long command chain and in what many people considered to have been an undesirable and unimportant position. As Flag Officer for U-boats (Führer der Unterseeboote), he held the ranks of Captain and Commodore and was responsible for running a small operational control department. This carried approximately the same authority as a cruiser captain. The real power in submarine command was wielded by the U-boat Division of the Supreme Naval Command in Berlin, with which Dönitz had virtually no contact. The U-boat Division did not seek his opinions and Dönitz did not influence submarine development, construction programmes, training schedules or naval policies. His isolation can be illustrated by the position of the submarine training flotilla which came under the jurisdiction of the Torpedo Inspectorate, and not under the Flag Officer for U-boats.

Dönitz's sole function was to prepare operational submarines for action and to employ them according to naval policy laid down by the Supreme Naval Command. To do this there were two types of instruction: general and specific. The idea was to follow the first mentioned until detailed directions were issued. The Navy did not have a policy for the deployment of submarines and in practice he received very little direct instructions. The emergency war programme, which came into effect on 15 August 1939, demanded all ships to put to sea, into pre-determined positions a long way from land, to prevent them being blockaded inside German ports. This had been rehearsed on at least four previous occasions and went off without difficulty. There was little for Dönitz to do since flotilla commanders were responsible for kitting out boats and the whole process ran almost automatically.

The German High Command had foreseen conflict in the Baltic, North Sea and in the Atlantic and therefore created the Three Front War Programme, which dictated that U-boats be directed from three operational control centres. Even by the first day of the Polish

September 1939 to May 1940

				OT	America to Africa		
				PQ	Iceland to North Russia		
				QP	North Russia to Iceland		
				RA	North Russia to Scotland		
				RS	Gibraltar to West Africa		
				SC	Halifax to United Kingdom		
				SL	Sierra Leone to United Kingdom		
				SR	West Africa to Gibraltar		
				TM	Trinidad to Gibraltar		
				TO	Africa to America		
				UC	United Kingdom to Caribbean		

CU	Caribbean to United Kingdom	**OG**	United Kingdom to Gibraltar
GUS	Gibraltar to North America	**ON**	United Kingdom to Norway and
HN	Norway to United Kingdon		later United Kingdom to North
HG	Gibraltar to United Kingdom		America
JW	Scotland to North Russia	**ONS**	United Kingdom to North
OB	United Kingdom to North		America (slow)
	America	**OS**	United Kingdom to West Africa

The suffix 'S' indicated a slow convoy and 'F' fast.

The major North Atlantic convoy routes.

Offensive though, it became clear that there would be no threat in the Baltic and the Three Front command system was abandoned. On 1 September 1939 Dönitz left the Baltic to set up his headquarters in a conglomeration of wooden huts in Sengwarden, on the landward side of Wilhelmshaven, where he took command of the North Sea and Atlantic. Two days after Britain and France declared war, the German government ordered offensive naval action with big ships to be curtailed but no instructions followed for U-boats at sea. So, Dönitz was free to employ them according to the general instructions which commanders had taken to sea in sealed en-

U35 (commissioned by FK Klaus Ewerth and later commanded by KK Werner Lott) manoeuvring in Wilhelmshaven harbour. Sticking up in front of the gun is the deck cover to the torpedo loading hatch. After sinking the freighter Diamantis *on 3 October 1939, Lott landed the crew near Dingle in County Kerry, Republic of Ireland. The Kaiser Wilhelm Swing Bridge is still operational today.*

velopes. A week later, he sought permission to bring a large number of U-boats home in order to prepare for an onslaught against merchant shipping. His argument was that Britain would most probably have prepared for a declaration of war by removing vulnerable targets from the sea. As there were no U-boats in reserve he thought it best to bring home those which had sailed in mid August and so have them ready when enemy wartime traffic emerged from its safe havens.

Although the events of the first months of the war have often been described, the true picture of the early problems has scarcely emerged. The frequently reported scenario suggests there was a concerted and harmonious action which began on the first day of the war with the sinking of the liner *Athenia* by U30 (KL Fritz-Julius Lemp). A more realistic view of the U-boat war can be obtained by looking at the often unreported events of U30's cruise.

Shortly after mid-day on 14 September, U30 chased and stopped the 5200-ton freighter *Fanad Head* and, complying with Prize Ordinance Regulation, towed the lifeboats away from the ship before dispatching a boarding party, under the leadership of the first watch officer (OL Hans-Peter Hinsch). Although U30 still had an adequate supply of fuel, there was a desperate shortage of food.

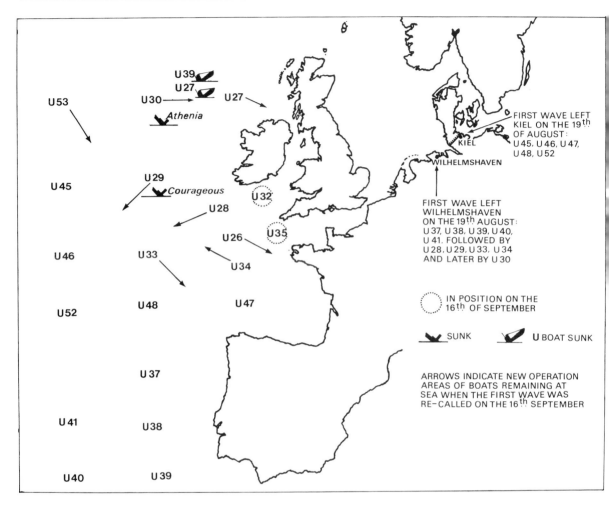

U-boat positions on 6 September 1939.

U26	FK	Oskar Schomburg
U27	KL	Johannes Franz
U28	KL	Günter Kuhnke
U29	KL	Otto Schuhart
U30	KL	Fritz-Julius Lemp
U32	OL	Hans Jenisch
U33	KL	Hans-Wilhelm von Dresky
U34	KL	Wilhelm Rollmann
U35	KL	Werner Lott
U37	KL	Heinrich Schuch
U38	KL	Heinrich Liebe
U40	KL	Werner von Schmidt
U41	KL	Gustav-Adolf Mugler
U45	KL	Alexander Gelhaar
U46	KL	Herbert Sohler
U47	KL	Günter Prien
U48	KL	Herbert Schultze
U52	KL	Wolfgang Barten
U53	KL	Ernst-Günther Heinicke

From left to right: Herbert Sohler (U46), Curt von Gossler (U49), Fritz-Julius Lemp (U30 & U110), Eitel Friedrich Kentrat (U8, U74 & U196) and Johannes Habekost (U31). Iron Crosses and U-boat badges indicate that this photo was taken some time after the start of the war, but there are no Knights Crosses. Lemp, the first of the group to receive his, had it awarded on 14 August 1940, so the picture was probably taken before that date.

The supply of tinned bread, loaded under the supervision of the radio operator (Georg Högel), turned out to have been wrongly labelled and upon opening the tins after their fresh bread began to go mouldy, the men found them to contain condensed milk. Therefore, Lemp ordered the boarding party to bring back any solid food they could find before sinking *Fanad Head* with scuttling charges and by opening the sea valves. U30 was facing the freighter, lying at rightangles to its side as three aircraft from HMS *Ark Royal* attacked. Two of them were brought down by the blast from their own bombs and, despite being injured himself, Matrosenobergefreiter Otto Ohse jumped into the water to save Flight Lieutenant Thursden, who was suffering from serious burns. Flight Lieutenant Guy Griffith (Royal Marines) managed to save himself by swimming to the freighter but the rest of the airmen perished. After considerable effort, Lemp managed to retrieve his boarding party and the two airmen. There had been some damage to the U30 and the first watch officer received slight injuries. The worst injury was to Maschinenmaat Adolf Schmidt who was bleeding from several shrapnel wounds in the head, back and arms and it looked as if he would die from a loss of blood. In an attempt to save his life, Lemp took the unorthodox step of requesting permission to sail to Iceland, where the German Consul, Professor Gerlach, was a distinguished doctor. By a twist of fate, after helping a U-boat man, he was killed by another. Apparently, he was a passenger aboard the liner *Arandora Star* when it was sunk by U47 (KL Günter Prien) in July 1940.

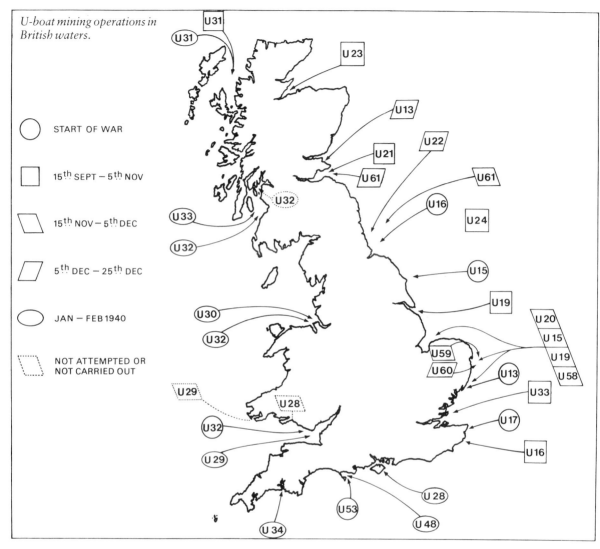

U-boat mining operations in British waters.

Legend:
- ○ START OF WAR
- □ 15th SEPT – 5th NOV
- ▱ 15th NOV – 5th DEC
- ▱ 5th DEC – 25th DEC
- ⬭ JAN – FEB 1940
- ⬭ (dotted) NOT ATTEMPTED OR NOT CARRIED OUT

Map labels: U31, U31, U23, U13, U22, U21, U61, U61, U32, U33, U16, U24, U32, U15, U19, U20, U15, U19, U58, U30, U59, U13, U32, U60, U33, U29, U28, U17, U32, U16, U29, U28, U53, U48, U34

At the beginning of the war:	**U33** KL Hans-Wilhelm von Dresky	**January to February 1940:**
U13 KL Karl Daublesky von Eichhain	*15 November to 5 December 1939:*	**U28** OL Friedrich Guggenberger
U15 KL Hein Buchholz	**U15** KL Peter Frahm	**U29** KL Otto Schuhart
U16 KL Udo Behrens	**U19** KL Wilhelm Müller-Arnecke	**U30** KL Fritz-Julius Lemp
U17 KL Harald Jeppener-Haltenhoff	**U20** KL Karl-Heinz Moehle	**U31** KL Johannes Habekost
U32 KL Paul Büchel	**U28** OL Friedrich Guggenberger	**U32** KK Paul Büchel
U53 KL Ernst-Günther Heinicke	**U58** KL Hans-Joachim Rahmlow	**U33** KL Hans-Wilhelm von Dresky
15 September to 5 November 1939:	**U59** KL Harald Jürst	**U34** KL Wilhelm Rollmann
U16 KL Horst Wellner	**U61** KL Jürgen Oesten	**U48** KL Herbert Schultze
U19 KL Hans Meckel	*5 to 25 December 1939:*	
U21 KL Fritz Frauenheim	**U13** KL Heinz Scheringer	
U23 KL Otto Kretschmer	**U22** KL Karl-Heinrich Jenisch	
U24 KL Harald Jeppener-Haltenhoff	**U60** KL Georg Schewe	
U31 KL Johannes Habekost		

When Lemp's arrival in Reykjavik became overdue, the operations room staff in Wilhelmshaven became worried. Short radio codes had not yet been introduced and U-boats were broadcasting lengthy messages in order to send vital information. Many officers were still convinced that Britain could determine the exact location of such transmissions and they expected U30 to have had a number of destroyers in hot pursuit. In the end, everything worked out well and U30 slipped into Reykjavik harbour on 19 September. Adolf Schmidt was handed over to consular staff and Lemp limped back into the vastness of the ocean. U30's engines had been showing signs of trouble for some time and now one of them gave out almost completely. Able to move only at slow speed, a minesweeper was sent out to escort U30 to safer waters. None of the problems described were unique to U30. The mechanical faults, common to all Type VIIA boats, were traced to weak engine mounts which needed urgent modification.

Every U-boat experienced difficulties with Prize Ordinance Regulations and Dönitz himself was not sure exactly what targets they should be aiming at. Following several requests to the Supreme Naval Command, the impractical and almost impossible restrictions were slowly lifted and this made things a little easier from October onwards. However, U-boats were not given a free hand to wage unrestricted warfare until August 1940.

Dönitz's promotion to Konteradmiral (Rear Admiral) in mid October, bringing with it the new title of Commander-in-Chief for U-boats, did not increase his autonomy. Rather, the opposite happened. Earlier, during the first week of the war, Grand Admiral Erich Raeder (Supreme Commander-in-Chief of the Navy) had stated that future submarine construction plans would be discussed with the Flag Officer for U-boats. Then, early in November, he sent Dönitz a terse memorandum in which he wrote, 'The Commander-in-Chief for U-boats is to devote his time to conducting battles at sea and he is not to occupy himself with technical matters'.

By November, technical failures had reached epidemic proportions. Not only boats, but also torpedoes showed signs of persistent weakness. At first the main difficulty lay in trying to find undisputable evidence of the causes for the reported failures. As early as August, Dönitz voiced concern over the functioning of torpedoes, but KA Oskar Wehr (chief of the Torpedo Trials Command (TEK) in Eckernförde) dismissed the matter by saying there was no evidence to support the claims. Yet, once the war started it did not take long for testimonies of failure to flood onto Dönitz's desk and

Fritz Drott enjoying the fresh air as U338 (KL Manfred Kinzel) runs into St Nazaire after the boat's first operational tour. The pennants attached to the partly raised attack periscope show the degree of their success, each one indicating a ship sunk, except the top one which signifies an aircraft shot down. There were no hard and fast rules about the hoisting of these flags and numerous variations were seen. For example, U99 (KK Otto Kretschmer) usually had its emblem, a horseshoe, painted on the flags. On the right is the raised rod aerial and on the left the commander's flagpole with his pennant. The barrels of machine guns can be seen sticking up.

by mid September there were ample examples of torpedoes passing under ships, exploding at the end of their runs or going off before reaching the target. To Dönitz, there appeared to be too many incidents to put them all down to war nerves. Something mechanical had to be wrong.

The Torpedo Inspectorate thought the magnetic detonation adjustment might be too sensitive and suggested a coarser setting, although it meant ships of less than 3000 tons would be too small to activate torpedoes with this setting. The revised instructions had just been broadcast to U-boats at sea, when U27 (KL Johannes Franz) was damaged by an explosion from his own torpedoes. The Torpedo Inspectorate responded by suggesting that the magnetic circuit be switched off and the contact detonator used instead. This was an easy matter, and could be carried out while torpedoes were lying in their tubes waiting to be fired, but the contact detonator was far less effective. A magnetic detonation under a merchant ship could result in it breaking its back and sinking quickly, but a hole in the side in no way guaranteed a sinking.

It was suggested that the premature explosions had been caused by a magnetic field created by cables inside the torpedo and this would not occur in new ones being delivered. Permission to use the magnetic circuit was re-instated during the second week of October 1939 but on the eighteenth of the month U46 (KL Herbert Sohler) radioed details of more premature explosions. At the same time, stories of torpedoes with contact detonators apparently passing under their targets increased. Dönitz remarked that U-boats faced much the same situation as in 1914, only then people knew how the primitive mechanisms worked but now the Torpedo Inspectorate did not seem to understand the problem.

Two days after the Torpedo Inspectorate had ordered the coarser settings, experts informed the U-boat Command that the contact pistol did not work because torpedoes were steering too deep. Dönitz reacted by telling commanders to adjust depth settings to two metres less than required, although he knew that such a setting would make it impossible to attack shallow draught ships. On 28 October 1939, there followed a meeting in Wilhelmshaven at which the Torpedo Inspectorate admitted that their experts did not know the exact reasons for premature explosions and said that they were looking into ways of stopping detonations at the end of torpedo runs. Less than a week later new detonators were available, and U28 (KL Günter Kuhnke) and U49 (KL Curt von Gossler) were equipped with them, but a fortnight later U49 started the flow of

failure reports. This was a bitter disappointment, shattering the U-boat Command's expectations, and it confirmed that Germany did not have an effective weapon for submarines.

Despite the entire U-boat offensive being apparently paralysed by ineffective torpedoes, not everyone accepted the statements made by commanders. The Torpedo Inspectorate, for example, claimed that premature explosions were no longer possible and that torpedoes must have been set off by wave action, and that this could be avoided if commanders went nearer to their targets. Dönitz however, replied by saying that U-boats were already close enough.

Despite the experience from the front, the Torpedo Inspectorate refused to recognise the problems, maintaining that everything was functioning well. On 17 January 1940, representatives of this body told the U-boat Command that failures were due to misses caused by poor aiming, and they further stated that the majority of the failures claimed could not be proved and that it was thus inappropriate to consider them. Dönitz rejected this out of hand, and

U405 near Narvik, inspecting a wreck from the earlier battles in that area. The partly extended rod aerial is on the left and the attack periscope on the right. The wires around it were intended to spiral the water and thus lessen the wake.

U30 (KL Fritz-Julius Lemp), shortly after mid-day on 14 September 1939, alongside the freighter Fanad Head.

following more tests, the Torpedo Inspectorate did acknowledge a fault and modified their regulations. Dönitz received these with the remark that torpedo failures were still the U-boats' biggest burden. At least 25 percent were duds, and this had resulted in about a hundred ships having been hit but not sunk. Postwar research has shown the failure rate to have been nearer 45 percent and it is interesting to note that U-boat commanders over-estimated the tonnage sunk by almost 30 percent. The U-boat Command had, therefore, a somewhat distorted picture of its successes.

During the first months of 1940, reports of premature explosions became less frequent, suggesting that the improvements had at last made an impact. However, the inconsistencies of the failures re-mained a puzzling feature. U50 (KL Max-Hermann Bauer) had one dud in 12, while an equally accomplished boat, U32 (KK Paul Büchel), experienced a 50 percent failure rate. The next crisis came during the Norwegian Campaign, when Dönitz received a high number of failure reports. With U47 (KL Günter Prien) claiming eight failures and both U46 (KL Herbert Sohler) and U25 (KK Victor Schütze) witnessing their torpedoes pass under their targets, Dönitz predicted a catastrophe in the narrow confines of the clear Norwegian fiords. After due consideration, but without clearing the matter with the Supreme Naval Command, he ordered the boats out of the fiords, into rougher, more open water, where they had a better chance of survival.

Midway through April, Dönitz said that successes at sea were not determined by the capabilities of the men or the boats, but by the reliability of torpedoes. He considered it absurd that the Commander-in-Chief for U-boats should spend so much of his time dealing with these technical problems, when he should be concentrating on fighting the war at sea. Yet he felt that he had to intervene when the appropriate authorities were apparently not doing their job. Professor E A Cornelius, appointed to study the problems, had only been on the job for a short time when he announced, 'There are too many failure possibilities with the detonators'. Following more inquiries, there emerged a worse picture than that which had been imagined by the U-boat Command. Apparently, the contact pistols had been tested only twice before the war and were declared operational despite having failed on both occasions. Dönitz considered such working practices to be criminally negligent. Even with his wide knowledge of torpedoes, Professor Cornelius was unable to pin-point all the defects and it was not until after the war that the Germans realised their problems had been caused by a combination of three errors. First, there were faults in the magnetic detonation system caused by bad designs which were not spotted until after the beginning of the war. Second, the build up of air pressure inside U-boats influenced the pressure sensitive depth setting apparatus and made torpedoes run too deep along erratic tracks. Last, the trigger prongs of the contact pistol were marginally smaller than the radius of the torpedo, which meant that though they were likely to detonate when hitting a deep-draught merchant ship at rightangles, they were prone to failure when hitting such a target at an acute angle or when encountering the shallow, curved hull of an escort. In such cases, the side of the torpedo instead of the prongs might contact the hull, causing it to be knocked out of line without exploding and then to continue along a new track.

Following the torpedo crisis of the beginning of the war, a number of modifications were made to the basic design, while other faults remained hidden. Although malfunctions were spotted by some commanders and reported in their logs, after the summer of 1940, the U-boat Command reckoned that their torpedoes were working quite effectively and did not easily accept that there were yet more serious problems. To make matters worse for Germany, the remaining problems did not really come to light until after the summer of 1943 when the new acoustic torpedoes were introduced. These torpedo failures during the early part of the war have often been referred to as The Torpedo Crisis and by that yardstick the

Of the 870 or so boats which left Germany for operational tours, some 550 sank nothing during the war. For these boats, the restless Atlantic was the biggest enemy.

later problems experienced with the acoustic torpedoes amounted to a catastrophe.

During the first winter of the war the problems experienced with torpedoes were partly offset by the use of mines, which played an important role in the German offensive and provided a lucrative alternative strategy during the long dark nights. There were two types of U-boat mine. The moored type was half the length of a torpedo and the other a third of a length, making it possible to carry two or three in one torpedo tube, and this was especially advantageous for the small Type II, which only had three bow tubes. Although a considerable number of mines could be stacked inside a U-boat, loading them during the laying of a barrage was considered too risky. Therefore, each operation with Type II boats was usually limited to dropping six to nine mines.

The U-boat Command's first major panic of the war concerned mining operations. This came about early in September when it was realised that U26 (KK Klaus Ewerth) might have been sunk in shallow waters off Portland and that the secret documents, which were on board, might have fallen into enemy hands. Dönitz immediately asked permission for U32 (KL Paul Büchel) to be diverted from Portsmouth to the Bristol Channel because fewer antisubmarine forces were thought to be in that area. A radio call instructed Büchel not to lock secret papers in his safe, but hide them where they would get wet – and the special ink dissolve – in the event of the boat sinking. Following this, many of the prewar mining plans were scrapped and a new offensive formulated. Earlier thinking had revolved around the idea of boats going out with mines and torpedoes, to act first as mine-layers before finding targets for the torpedoes. Following the realisation that secrets might have inadvertently been passed to the enemy, the U-boat Command decided that it would be better for boats going out into shallow waters with mines to carry only enough documentation for the one trip. Though this restricted them to a single objective, it was thought preferable to risking the loss of vital papers which could put other boats at risk.

2. Return to the Atlantic after Norway

For Dönitz, the invasion of Norway started on 4 March 1940 when the Supreme Naval Command ordered departures to be cancelled and boats at sea, including KL Dietrich Knorr (U51) who had just left Kiel, to be recalled. That day marked the start of a severely restricted period for the U-boat Command, when schedules devised by higher authorities made it necessary to curtail usual operations. Little was sunk as submarines were used principally as escorts, weather stations, cargo carriers and for patrolling empty seas. To make matters worse, the Royal Navy captured a map showing German dispositions and thus managed to avoid most U-boats, and the majority of British ships which were unfortunate enough to fall within the range of attack were saved by torpedo failures.

May to September 1940

Dönitz disagreed with many of the tasks which were assigned to U-boats, believing that they would be better employed against shipping rather than given over to the more passive tasks off Norway. This disagreement emphasised the wide rift between the U-boat Command and the naval leadership. On several occasions, Dönitz's staff restrained him from going for a showdown with their superiors. The men felt that open conflict with the hierarchy would only result in worse conditions than those which were already being experienced. It was feared that the U-boat Command might lose some of its autonomy and that more boats might be put under the control of other naval authorities. His annoyance would have probably been worse had he been acquainted with more details of the plans being put forward by Supreme Naval Command. During the middle of April, for example, Grand Admiral Erich Raeder offered to divert new front boats from the U-boat Command to be converted into freighters, though these plans for supplying the Army and Air Force in Norway did not go ahead. Prospects of re-establishing other reliable links to the north such as road, rail and coastal transport increased after the consolidation of the German occupation and the Supreme Command of the Armed Forces (OKW) chose alternative forms of transport.

Though of only short duration, the Norwegian offensive in-volved many boats in intensive activity, resulting in long queues at the repair yards. There, the shortage of skilled labour further aggravated delays and it was not until the middle of May that the

As air raids became an ever increasing threat to the French bases, steps were taken to camouflage headquarters. This appears to be part of the 9th Flotilla complex.

first boats ventured back into the shipping lanes. Another four weeks had to pass before this spearhead was reinforced with sufficient numbers for establishing patrol lines. The three months' absence from the Atlantic had given Dönitz great cause for concern. What changes had taken place? Were there still lone ships or had all shipping been bunched into convoys? What routes were being followed? Where did convoys assemble? What changes had taken place in the escort patterns? What about air cover? On top of these questions, there was a genuine worry about the morale of the U-boat crews. Having experienced near mutinies earlier in his career, Dönitz now recognised similar conditions and he was not certain how well the rank and file had withstood the depressing failures in Norway. Confidence could only be restored, he felt, with the introduction of new torpedoes, but for the time being any meagre successes were urgently required to bridge the gap.

The new offensive started, however, with depressing news. KL Victor Oehrn (U37), which left on 15 May to become the first boat to return to the Atlantic after Norway, started by dominating the air waves with descriptions of four torpedo failures. Dönitz told KS Eberhard Godt (chief of the operations department), 'What a start! We cannot burden the men with this misery for a second time and it will be better to get a few rotten successes than none at all. Prohibit the use of magnetic detonators and let us hope the contact pistols

January 1942. U586 (KL Dietrich von der Esch) with Paul Preuss helping to load stores shortly before the first operational tour. All packages had to be less than half a metre wide to fit through the narrow hatches which were situated in the ceilings of the boats' compartments.

will produce some results'. Then came an unexpected and valuable boost. U37 returned to Wilhelmshaven on 9 June, having sunk 11 ships of 43,000 GRT in 26 days at sea. (The postwar figure is given as 11 ships of 50,701 GRT.) The news that the dreadful spell had been broken was a terrific morale booster, and reached the majority of the crews before they started their offensive in June 1940. U37's successes marked the beginning of a completely new era in submarine warfare which was to have a most shattering effect on Britain.

✻   ✻   ✻

By the time this new offensive started, there had been important changes in the basic configuration of both sides. On the German front, access to the Norwegian coast provided new and much-needed facilities. Though a long distance from British shipping lanes, the Norwegian ports offered safe havens for repairs while access to and from the Norwegian coast was safer than that to and from German ports. The dangers of attacks in the hazardous German coastal waters were highlighted by incidents like the submarine attack on U122 (KL Hans Günther Looff) while on passage out of Kiel during the middle of the May. An acute shortage of escorts and minesweepers meant that most U-boats had to travel unescorted through the narrow coastal channels.

After torpedo failures, mechanical breakdowns were the second biggest cause of worry. Many boats developed faults during their first few days at sea, and Dönitz welcomed the opportunity of being able to use Norwegian facilities to carry out small but vital repairs. Most of these problems were blamed on poor workmanship in the repair yards and Dönitz considered the delays intolerable, particularly when these breakdowns prevented the formation of a wolf pack during May 1940. The problems were varied. For instance, U28 (KL Günter Kuhnke) and U29 (KL Otto Schuhart) were forced back by engine trouble, while U48 (KK Hans Rösing) had to return after one of the hatches was found to be leaking and U65 (KK Hans Gerrit von Stockhausen) put into Bergen with a leaking welded seam.

The German occupation of France in June 1940 was the most significant event at this stage of the war, and provided access to the Atlantic coast, while the active co-operation of the French helped to increase the effectiveness of the U-boats. Return journeys from the convoy routes were shortened by some 900 nautical miles (1650 km) or a minimum of four days' sailing, assuming that there were no interruptions from the enemy, and assistance from French shipyard workers reduced the turn-round time in port by almost 22 percent. Up until this time two and a half boats had been in port for every submarine at sea and the French helped to reduce this figure to a ratio of 1.8:1 The popular image is of men working for the Germans at gun point, and the majority of French people belonging to the underground resistance. But this is not altogether true. Much of the work was too skilled to be carried out by forced labour and, on the whole, French workers enjoyed quite a number of benefits. Indeed, there is evidence that they worked a great deal better than many of their counterparts in Germany.

The proximity of Great Britain and the awkwardness of the geographical location made the invasion an almost exclusively Army and Air Force offensive, with the Navy undertaking only a few minor tasks along the Dutch and Belgian coasts. This allowed the officers of the U-boat Command a freer hand than they had had during the Norwegian Campaign and during this period they were able to formulate their own plans. Dönitz was quick in exploiting this situation.

The invasion provided Dönitz with two opportunities. First, there was, as mentioned earlier, the prospect of using the French Atlantic ports and harbours and, second, and more immediately, Dönitz calculated that the presence of the German army around

Calais would force cross-channel traffic further west, where journey times would be longer and conditions better for attacks with
Type VII boats. Though the western Channel lay within short flying
time of Germany, it was difficult to gain information about shipping and so two U-boats, U28 (KL Günter Kuhnke) and U101 (KL
Fritz Frauenheim), were dispatched to reconnoitre. After two days
at sea, Kuhnke turned back to Trondheim for engine repairs and
was replaced by U29 (KL Otto Schuhart). U101 and U29 aimed for
the Cherbourg, Le Havre, Dieppe area, but fog prevented any
action and finally the U-boat Command ordered them to move on
to the northwest of Spain.

Dönitz had little intelligence information about the French Atlantic coast and early in June 1940 he sent KKdr (der Reserve) Helmut
Brümmer-Patzig and KL (Ing) (Engineer) Hans Looschen overland
to carry out a general reconnaissance of possible bases and at the
same time a train was loaded with the necessary materials to
provision and repair U-boats. This complicated task of creating a
temporary, self-contained support unit, with personnel from the
naval dockyard in Wilhelmshaven, was carried out under the
supervision of KS Clamor von Trotha, who was also responsible for
moving the waggons first to Paris and later on to Lorient.

Following a visit on 23 June to west France for a personal
evaluation Dönitz concluded that it would be best to provide
facilities in stages. Having selected Lorient as the first base, the
primary aim was to provide fuel, lubricating oil, water, food,
ammunition and other small commodities. Minor repairs were to
be taken on at the next stage, and that was to be followed by moving
the entire operations department. The final step was to provide
facilities for major repair work.

On the whole, these plans worked well although events did not
take place as planned. Brümmer-Patzig was appointed provisional
commander in Lorient and the first U-boat, U30 (KL Fritz-Julius
Lemp), arrived on 7 July 1940, the day after the port was declared
open. Preparations then continued throughout the summer and on
2 August Lorient was declared fully operational. However, moving
the operations department was more difficult. It necessitated laying
telephone and telex cables for easy connection with Kiel, Wilhelmshaven and Berlin, and the complications incurred meant that the
headquarters had to be moved in stages, with an interim office in
Boulevard Suchet (Paris) from September to November 1940. Full
operational control was switched at mid-day on 29 August 1940
and Dönitz arrived there during the afternoon.

*Tirpitz Mole, position 32 or 33,
at the Naval Harbour in Kiel
with U46 under Engelbert
Endrass, who fired the
torpedoes against the battleship
Royal Oak in Scapa Flow when
he was First Watch Officer of
U47 (KL Günter Prien). U46
had a number of commanders,
among them Herbert Sohler,
later Chief of the 7th U-Flotilla
and OL Konstantin von
Puttkamer, who should not be
confused with Karl-Jesko von
Puttkamer, naval adjutant at
the Führer's headquarters.*

Men from U377 posing for a photograph with the headquarters of the 9th U-boat Flotilla (Brest) in the background.

Right: Commander-in-Chief for U-boats at Kerneval in France during the summer of 1940. Dönitz frequently spent time with his men in order to keep his finger on the pulse.

A brief visit by Dönitz to Lorient during the first week of September revealed several problems. Recreation accommodation was urgently required for men coming from hard operations and a large mansion at Quiberon was employed to meet immediate needs. At this time, mines were considered to be the worst hazard that U-boats were to encounter and requests were made to provide the best possible sweeping service. The Royal Air Force also left its mark when five planes flew over Lorient and bombed the yard from less than 1000 feet (300 metres). Their aiming was inaccurate and the explosions were barely audible to men inside the submarines, but this unwelcome interruption clearly demonstrated that anti-aircraft armament needed strengthening.

There were several other important events during the August of 1940 that are worth recording. On the seventeenth, Hitler declared a total blockade area around the British Isles in which U-boats were permitted to attack shipping without warning, thus making operations considerably easier. As the move to France had increased the efficiency of the boats it was realised that the torpedo forecasts, made when submarines were operating on the long routes from Germany, were out-of-date. Raeder had to pay a special visit to

Hitler requesting production to be stepped up, explaining that the U-boat operations would be seriously curtailed and all advantages of the French coast lost if this was not done.

Also in August came the unpleasant realisation that British ships were managing to avoid U-boats. Two steps were taken to combat this. First, commanders were instructed not to use their radio, except for urgent sighting reports and, second, a spy hunt was started in the U-boat Command. This resulted in the unfortunate effect of numbers being reduced just at a time when the staff should have been expanded to cope with the escalation of the U-boat war.

Unreliable radios presented further problems. U25 (KL Heinz Beduhn) and U46 (KL Engelbert Endrass) were given up as sunk and aircraft from the Luftwaffe Command at Brest were sent out to look for survivors. As it turned out, U25 had been lost on a mine whilst travelling from Wilhelmshaven to Lorient, while Endrass was alive and well, cursing the broken radio equipment. On this occasion the spare parts were not yet available in France and the boat left again for another mission without the use of its short wave transmitter.

*   *   *

The potential dangers posed by the presence of British submarines off the French coast and the unreliability of the U-boat radios led Dönitz, in the summer of 1940, to establish a special signal station on the Isle de Groix, outside Lorient, with which U-boats without radios could establish visual contact before being escorted through the protective mine field. The R-boats (small minesweepers, which looked like motor torpedo boats without torpedo tubes) were only suitable for escort duty during reasonably calm weather and so the U-boat Command requested Sperrbrecher *Rostock* to be sent out from Germany. She was a modified freighter, designed to detonate mines without sinking and intended to lead the way through dangerous waters. It is important to emphasise here that Dönitz was the commander of a small unit and the services of other navy departments did not automatically follow U-boats to France.

It has often been maintained that British submarines and mines in French coastal waters played only a minor role during this part of the war. But the reverse is true. In September 1940, these two factors played a part which still today has scarcely been recognised. The sinking of the Luftwaffe's catapult ship *Ostmark* on the fourteenth led Dönitz to tell his staff, 'It will not be long before the entire U-boat fleet is lost on our own doorstep'. Anxious to learn whether U-boats succeeded in crossing the Bay of Biscay, he ordered them to send a confirmation once they reached ten degrees west (later, fifteen degrees west). Having identified this signal, British Intelligence used it as their first step in tracking U-boats. Each transmission became a flag on the secret submarine tracking room's map. Since it was possible to determine the approximate latitude of the transmission, Rodger Winn (head of the Admiralty's secret submarine tracking room) later used this to predict whether the boat was going into the convoy routes of the North Atlantic, to America or into southern waters. In later years, it became an important tool in helping to focus Bay Air Patrols.

Joining in the war on Germany's side on 10 June 1940, the Italian Naval Command requested permission to share facilities on the French Atlantic coast. Dönitz considered the Italian naval structure to be somewhat antiquated and did not want to enter into negotiations which might result in the Italians asking for control of German submarines in the Mediterranean. Therefore, he declined to accept their submarines under his command and suggested an autonomous Italian U-boat headquarters be established in France. Following a visit from KA Angelo Parona on 10 August 1940, Bordeaux was chosen as the base. Minesweeping, anti-aircraft cover, port protection duties and telephone and telex systems were provided by the German Navy, while both sides supplied liaison officers to ensure smooth co-operation.

While Dönitz and the U-boat Command were digging in for a long, hard offensive, senior staff in Germany were taking a slightly different view. U-boat construction was running nowhere near the optimum, repairs were slow because skilled workers were being called up to the armed forces and naval resources were stretched beyond the limit while attempting to protect a coastline from Spain to the north of Norway. Yet during the summer of 1940 Grand Admiral Erich Raeder and Hitler devoted considerable time to discussing plans for the future peacetime fleet. Both men were hoping that the half hearted attempt of trying to assemble an invasion fleet in the Channel ports would scare the British into peace negotiations. It was only the British government's declaration to fight on at all cost, combined with the Luftwaffe's failure during the Battle of Britain which forced a considerable shifting of the scenery for the next act of the war at sea. After almost a year of war, thoughts of a future peacetime fleet were put aside and attention firmly focused on the U-boat war in the Atlantic convoy routes.

3. Strike Against Convoys

By August 1940, U-boats were operating up to 800 miles west of Ireland, while the limit of convoy escorts was only half that distance. Convoys to America were accompanied out to about 17 degrees west and then continued as a group for one more day before dispersing. Meanwhile, escorts went off to rendezvous with an incoming group of merchant ships. An ocean escort, usually an armed merchant ship, sometimes accompanied the convoy through the mid-Atlantic region. This simple-sounding arrangement was, however, fraught with frustrations. Even a brief delay in schedules, for instance, could result in warships running short of fuel and having to break their missions at crucial times. When Halifax, Nova Scotia, the western assembly point for convoys, became too over-crowded, Sydney on the eastern side of Cape Breton Island was chosen as an alternative rendezvous for slower ships. From there, the Atlantic crossing usually entailed a voyage of 16 days for the slow SC convoys, travelling at up to eight knots, and ten days for the fast HX routes. The normal southward bound convoys from Britain were usually escorted all the way to Gibraltar because they passed closer to U-boat bases. A special anti-submarine escort accompanied the group as far as the latitude on which Lorient lies and from there one, two or sometimes three small warships would sail with the merchantmen until they were met by forces from Gibraltar. Since Britain did not have a great deal of choice in deciding on convoy routes and could only add slight variation to the patterns, it was easy for the U-boat Command to establish where convoys were likely to be.

*　　*　　*

After the Norwegian Campaign, Dönitz started to become impatient. After almost a year of war he had still not been able to play his trump card – the wolf pack attack. An opportunity came in early June 1940, after the cancellation of the emergency plans for the invasion of Norway. The long queues at the repair yards actually helped Dönitz to realise his plans because instead of there being many boats at sea or returning home there were a great number now slowly emerging from the yards: enough to form two wolf packs.

GROUP RÖSING, against convoy US3,
12–15 June.

U48	KK	Hans Rösing	VIIB
U29	KL	Otto Schuhart	VIIA
U43	KL	Wilhelm Ambrosius	IXA
U46	KL	Engelbert Endrass	VIIB
U101	KL	Fritz Frauenheim	VIIB

GROUP PRIEN, against convoy HX48,
12–15 June.

U47	KL	Günter Prien	VIIB
U25	KL	Heinz Beduhn	IA
U28	KL	Günter Kuhnke	VIIA
U30	KL	Fritz-Julius Lemp	VIIA
U32	OL	Hans Jenisch	VIIA
U38	KL	Heinrich Liebe	IXA
U51	KL	Dietrich Knorr	VIIB

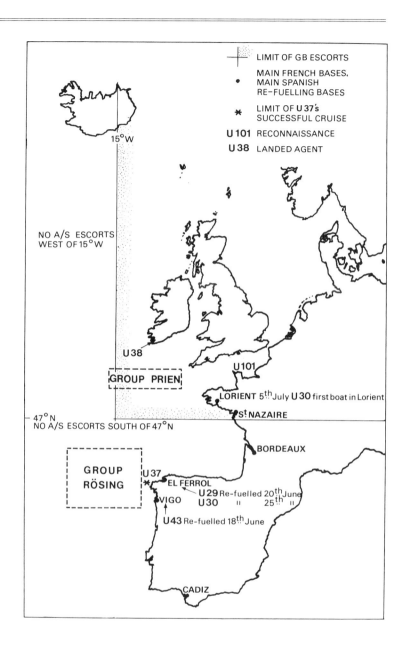

*U-boat operation: May to June
1940.*

The first wolf pack or patrol line, Group RÖSING (named after the tactical commander KK Hans Rösing, who as Chief of the 7th U-Flotilla had taken over U48 when Herbert Schultze was taken ill), was set up west of Cape Finisterre to intercept a northward-bound convoy, US3, which had been detected by the B-Dienst (Radio Monitoring Service). The course was not known and therefore the chances of getting a shot at it were thin. Furthermore, the U-boat Command had identified it as consisting of troop transports with heavy escorts, which probably made it too fast for shadowing U-boats. Nevertheless, it was too important a target to ignore. The second patrol line, Group PRIEN, was established in the western approaches to the English Channel, where convoy HX48 was expected.

Neither of these two convoys was sighted, although the majority of U-boats did quite well by sinking lone ships, which were still in great abundance. In fact, U47 (KL Günter Prien) returned to Kiel on 6 July claiming to have sunk ten ships, totalling 66,587 GRT, making the cruise the most successful of the war to date. Postwar research by Professor Jürgen Rohwer has shown the correct total to be eight ships totalling 51,483 GRT.

U100 (KK Joachim Schepke). The sinking of U47 (KK Günter Prien), U70 (KK Joachim Matz), U99 (KK Otto Kretschmer) and U100 in the spring of 1941 marked the turning point in the Battle of the Atlantic. The railing running the full length of the upper deck and the background details suggest that this photograph was taken during trials off Kiel and it can therefore be dated around the summer of 1940.

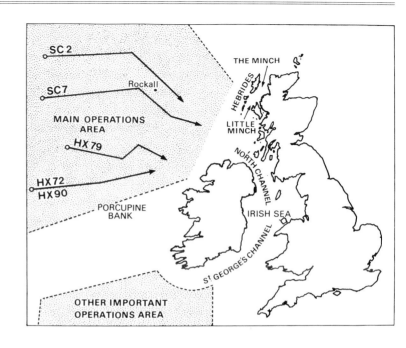

U-boat operations: September to December 1940.

The battle against 53 ships of convoy SC2 during the first week of September 1940.
The first successful group operation.

U28	KL	Günter Kuhnke
U47	KL	Günter Prien
U65	KK	Hans-Gerrit von Stockhausen
U99	KL	Otto Kretschmer
U101	KL	Fritz Frauenheim

41 ships of convoy HX72 were sighted on 20 September 1940 by U47:

U29	KL	Otto Schuhart
U32	OL	Hans Jenisch
U46	KL	Engelbert Endrass
U47	KL	Günter Prien
U48	KL	Heinrich Bleichrodt
U65	KL	Hans-Gerrit von Stockhausen
U99	KL	Otto Kretschmer
U100	KL	Joachim Schepke
U138	OL	Wolfgang Lüth

30 ships of convoy SC7 were sighted on 17 October 1940 by U48 (KL Heinrich Bleichrodt) and the following were directed towards it:

U38	KL	Heinrich Liebe
U46	KL	Engelbert Endrass
U99	KL	Otto Kretschmer
U100	KL	Joachim Schepke
U101	KL	Fritz Frauenheim
U123	KL	Karl-Heinz Moehle

Convoy HX79 was sighted on 19 October by U47 (KL Günter Prien) and boats from SC7 plus the following made an attempt to find it:

| U28 | KL | Günter Kuhnke |
| U48 | KL | Heinrich Bleichrodt |

Also on 19 October, three other boats:

U46	KL	Engelbert Endrass
U93	KL	Claus Korth
U124	KL	Wilhelm Schulz

chased OB229.

The action against convoys SC7 and HX79 was the most successful convoy battle in terms of the number of ships sunk per participating U-boat.

Plans for refuelling in Spanish waters started to pay dividends for the RÖSING Group. Before the facilities in France were established, at least four boats managed to slip into either El Ferrol or Vigo instead of making the long return journeys to Germany. They were supplied by German freighters especially placed in out-of-the-way positions for the purpose of provisioning U-boats. The occupation of the French Atlantic ports made the replenishment points in northern Spain unnecessary, and also made it possible to bring smaller submarines (Type II) into the Atlantic shipping lanes. The first major movement of these coastal boats took place towards the beginning of July when a group sailed from Bergen in Norway to North Channel (between Ireland and Scotland) and Minch in the Hebrides. Some of these boats then continued southwards to Lorient for further operations in the convoy routes. The concentration of merchant shipping in North Channel made it an attractive area for Dönitz to send U-boats to and another two waves were sent there before the end of the year. Results were somewhat mediocre, with torpedo failures still dominating the first operations.

Meanwhile, further out in the Atlantic, attacks were concentrated mainly on single ships sailing on their own but occasionally on convoys when they ran into the path of a U-boat. The first really successful group attack started on 30 August, after the B-Dienst

U99 (KL Otto Kretschmer). This interesting photograph of the conning tower, looking forward, shows the attack periscope with a signal pistol on the left and a signal lamp on the right. The compass attached to the periscope mount has a sighting device attached to it and the special binoculars are attached to the torpedo aimer. The first watch officer was responsible for shooting torpedoes on the surface. At first, it was necessary to aim the whole boat at the target, but in later years deflection apparatus was incorporated into the shooting equipment.

(Radio Monitoring Service) decoded details of the eastern meeting point of anti-submarine escorts and convoy SC2. Having obtained this news four days before the event, four U-boats were ordered to the spot at 57°00′North 19°50′West. The Supreme Naval Command reduced this number to three by insisting one submarine be stationed in mid-Atlantic to act as weather station. Convoy SC2 was first sighted by U65 (KL Hans-Gerrit von Stockhausen) shortly after the escorts arrived, putting the U-boats at considerable disadvantage. This was immediately demonstrated when the destroyer *Skeena* and corvette *Periwinkle* forced U65 away. Being rather short of small anti-submarine vessels, the Admiralty had instructed escorts to return to the convoy as soon as possible and therefore neither of these two ships pursued the U-boat, making it possible for U65 to relocate the convoy a few hours later.

According to prewar rehearsals, U65's most important task was to remain with the convoy, sending regular course details and, if requested, radio beacon signals. These made it possible for U47 (KL Günter Prien) to locate the convoy and sink three ships in 90 minutes just before daylight on 7 September. Further attacks were frustrated by aircraft, which forced both submarines into the cellar. However, U47 and U65 resurfaced soon afterwards to continue with their hunt, getting within range at dusk during the following

A convoy at sea. Of the 1100 or so U-boats which were built, less than half came as close as this to an enemy convoy. Paul Popper

night, when U28 (KL Günter Kuhnke) and U99 (KL Otto Kretschmer) also reached the scene.

Prien, who had only one torpedo left, was ordered to relieve U124 as weather station at 23° West because her torpedo doors had jammed. This monotonous job required the boat to remain in a fixed position in order to broadcast meteorological data twice a day. Dönitz objected most strongly, maintaining that operational boats should not be used for such tasks, when they could be doing more productive work. The crews at sea did not like such a passive role either, considering themselves to be sitting targets for enemy radio detection stations. However, this fear was not really well-founded. A few days later 41 ships of convoy HX72 sailed close by U47, unaware of its presence, only a short time after the ocean escort, the auxiliary cruiser, *Jervis Bay*, had left them.

The 20 September was an especially frustrating day for Prien. Though the convoy took priority over the weather reporting, as first boat on the scene, he was not allowed to shoot his last torpedo. Instead, his standing orders instructed him to sail ahead of the ships, reporting their movements. Otto Kretschmer (U99), being close at hand, lost no time in hitting three ships during the first night. One of these was only damaged by the torpedo, to be sunk later by gunfire from U47. KL Joachim Schepke improved on U99's effort by going in for two attacks during the following night. On the first occasion all four bow torpedoes were shot in less than five minutes. The wolf pack was beginning to make an impression and convoy HX72 might well have been decimated further had the other U-boats not been short of torpedoes.

The U-boat Command put the successes down to three important factors. First, the eastward bound convoy was detected far west with only a few escorts. Second, all participating boats behaved according to principles laid down during their training. Third, the weather was favourable. Dönitz added that the successes demonstrated that their peacetime ideas on convoy attacks had been correct and he emphasised that five boats, almost 400 nautical miles apart, had been successfully brought together for this operation.

Two days before Prien sighted convoy HX72, there was the attack on the 11081-GRT Ellerman Liner, *City of Benares*, resulting in the loss of almost 80 children. U48's commander, KL Heinrich Bleichrodt, had no way of knowing that his target contained so many children and long after the war he was still upset by the incident.

Exactly one month after sighting the *City of Benares*, U48 was instrumental in starting the most successful convoy battle of the whole war (success being measured according to tonnage sunk per participating U-boat). The success came about from a combination of five U-boats, each with almost a full load of torpedoes, intercepting thirty east-bound ships of convoy SC7 a long way west. On having received U48's sighting report, the U-boat Command ordered a wolf pack of five boats to intercept. (These were U46, KL Engelbert Endrass; U99, KL Otto Kretschmer; U100, KL Joachim Schepke; U101, Kl Fritz Frauenheim; and U123, KL Karl-Heinz Moehle.) Although U38 (KL Heinrich Liebe) managed to make two attacks during the night of 17/18 October, it only succeeded in sinking one ship and on both occasions was driven off by the escorts, which had joined the convoy shortly before U48 sighted it. However, the escorts failed to drive off the attack by the wolf pack during the following night and all five boats managed to get in within range, to sink some 16 ships and damage one more without loss or significant damage to a single U-boat.

A coastal convoy under air attack. Paul Popper

Dönitz in France.

To make matters worse for Britain, while trying to home in on U48's convoy, KL Günter Prien (U47) sighted 49 ships of convoy HX79, and another five U-boats, which were too far away to reach convoy SC7, were called in to help U47. This attack started shortly after 2200 hours on the night of 19 October. Conditions were right for the utter confusion and devastation of the previous night to repeat itself. Four U-boats sunk most of the 12 ships with two more U-boats, both short on torpedoes, carrying out mopping up work with their guns.

Dönitz described it as a great success, adding that the action had proved his controversial prewar training for night time, short-range attacks to have been correct. In addition, he recognised that the developments in radio telegraphy since World War I had made the whole operation possible. Other important points in his diary stressed the necessity of the boats being in the battlefield before the convoy arrived; there being enough boats to cover a wide enough area and the need for favourable weather. He concluded by noting that the determining factor would always be the ability of each individual U-boat commander and that successes were only possible as a result of the essential and comprehensive training schedules which the commander and crew had undergone.

U143 (KL Ernst Mengersen), a long-range coastal boat of Type IID, 21 October 1940. The boat had been in service for only a few weeks, which suggests that the periscope might have been bent during training, rather than in action. With the availability of French bases, a number of this small type were employed in the waters to the west of the British Isles. The deck gun is of 20mm calibre.

For the British, these successes represented a setback. Asdic, the new wonder device for detecting submerged submarines, in which the Admiralty had put so much faith before the war, was useless against surfaced U-boats. Convoy escorts had to rely on visual sightings and the small conning towers were almost invisible at night. To make matters worse, the vast majority of the escorts could not muster enough speed to catch a surfaced U-boat. The Royal Navy was not prepared for surface attacks and had to pay dearly for this neglect. Countermeasures did not start to make an impact until the spring of 1941 and the months from June and throughout the autumn of 1940 were indeed the U-boats' most successful time, often referred to as the Happy or Golden Time.

It seems strange that Britain was so unprepared for Dönitz's offensive, since the surface attack strategy was by no means new. The surface attack at night had already been pioneered in 1916, when the Imperial Navy had used submarines as torpedo boats, and in 1939 Dönitz had written a book in which he outlined his views on future submarine actions. In addition, during prewar exercises the Royal Navy used the surface attack with good results, but when the war started it was taken by surprise and the merchant navy had to pay the price.

The Italians, who moved into Bordeaux during August 1940, made a disappointing contribution to the convoy battles. Though there were a few noteworthy individual successes, they made no significant overall impact. It was not that the men failed in their task, but simply that the training and general attitudes were unsuited for the rigours of the Atlantic. They had been trained for short duration attacks against enemy harbours and for submerged attacks. By the end of 1940, Dönitz had written off any hope of utilising the Italians for any planned offensive, and told his staff that they would be best sent to areas where they could not interfere with German operations.

The first major bone of contention was aired towards the end of September when Dönitz suggested the Italian boats be sent out for the longest possible time, to return only when their supplies had been exhausted, instead of going out for a pre-determined period of two to three weeks. Agreement could not be reached, and finally the Italians compromised by keeping the boats at sea for an additional three days. To the further annoyance of the Germans, two weeks later an Italian boat reported a convoy, but neither speed nor course was given and apparently no attempt made to pursue the merchant ships.

Dönitz's main aim was to inflict the greatest possible damage on Britain and he considered everything else to be subordinate to this. Any assistance to achieve this objective was vital. During the first week of November 1940 he tried to convince VA Angelo Parona of the importance of adopting the German methods of working, while retaining their maximum freedom in the operations. He wanted the men to feel they were commanded by Italians, not Germans. Dönitz suggested they could make up for inadequacies in their training by sending men to the commanders' school at Gotenhafen and giving them the opportunity of going out with German boats. Finally, it was also agreed to increase the German staff in Bordeaux, with KK Hans Rösing as main liaison officer.

4. The Long Hard Winter

November 1940 to February 1941

Preparations for moving the U-boat Command from Paris to the Atlantic coast took longer than anticipated and it was not until 11 November 1940 that control was switched to Kerneval near Lorient. The seasonal bad weather brought an expected reduction in tonnage sunk, but this was not serious enough to consider alternative operations areas in calmer regions. Overall results in the South Atlantic were too disappointing for further action to be considered. Therefore, the North Western Approaches and North Channel remained the favourite hunting grounds for the U-boat Command.

Dönitz was against spreading U-boats over too large an area and had always advocated employing them in the most favourable places as close to their bases as possible. The example of UA (KL Hans Cohausz) operating with auxiliary cruiser *Pinguin* (KS Ernst-Felix Krüder) in the South Atlantic demonstrated the uselessness of sending boats to far-off waters and this was later confirmed by KK Hans-Gerrit von Stockhausen (U65) who sank only eight ships during the six-month-long tour (counting from start of preparations to end of overhaul afterwards) in the Freetown area off West Africa. Dönitz felt the two boats would have achieved much more if they had joined a patrol line in the North Atlantic. This negative view of the South Atlantic changed somewhat towards the end of February 1941, when U65 returned and it was realised that U-boat Command had positioned the boat some distance from the main British shipping routes.

*   *   *

The U-boat Command had established itself in the new headquarters at Kerneval by mid January 1941 when Dönitz took his annual leave. The usual reduction in activity during the seasonal poor weather had already established winter holidays as part of the routine. This time he went away with the disturbing news that convoys seemed to be avoiding wolf packs and when he returned he found the theory confirmed. This was particularly worrying because finding convoys, the biggest problem which had been encountered during the previous summer, had not yet been solved and now

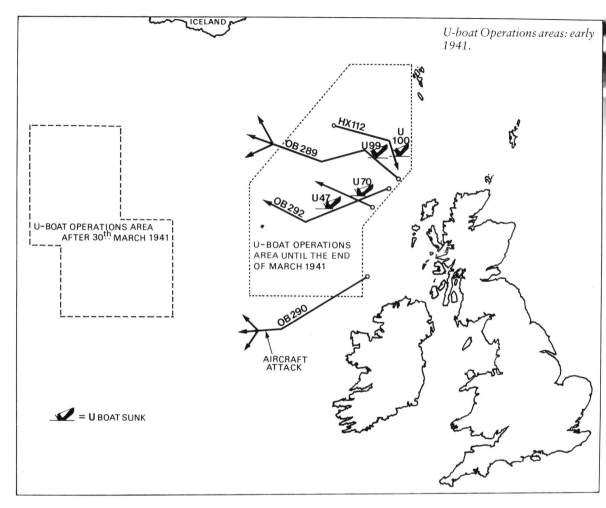

U-boat Operations areas: early 1941.

ICELAND

HX112

OB 289

U99

U 100

U70

U47

OB 292

U-BOAT OPERATIONS AREA
AFTER 30th MARCH 1941

U-BOAT OPERATIONS
AREA UNTIL THE END
OF MARCH 1941

OB 290

AIRCRAFT
ATTACK

= U BOAT SUNK

22 February, convoy OB288 was sighted by aircraft from IKG40 and the following boats ordered into a patrol line:

U69	KL	Jost Metzler
U73	KL	Helmut Rosenbaum
U96	KL	Heinrich Lehmann-Willenbrock
U97	KL	Udo Heilmann
U107	KK	Günter Hessler
U552	KK	Erich Topp
Barbarigo	CC	Giulio Ghiglieri (Italian)
Bianchi	CC	Adalberto Giovannini (Italian)

23 February, convoy OB289 sighted by U552 (KL Erich Topp) and

U95	KL	Gerd Schreiber
U97	KL	Udo Heilmann
U108	KK	Klaus Scholtz

were directed towards it.

25 February, convoy OB290 was sighted by U47 (KL Günter Prien). A number of U-boats were directed towards it, but they failed to make contact. Five aircraft from IKG40 attacked. The battle resulted in the greatest single success by aircraft.

6 March, convoy OB293 was sighted by U47 (KL Günter Prien).

U70	KL	Joachim Matz
U99	KL	Otto Kretschmer

UA	KL	Hans Eckermann
U74	KL	Eitel-Friedrich Kentrat

managed to make contact. U37 (KL Clausen) did not manage to reach the merchant ships. UA was damaged and U47 and U70 were sunk.

15 March, convoy HX112 sighted by U110 (KL Fritz-Julius Lemp).

U37	KL	Nicolai Clausen
U74	KL	Eitel-Friedrich Kentrat
U99	KL	Otto Kretschmer
U100	KL	Joachim Schepke

reach the convoy. U99 and U100 were sunk.

it appeared that the enemy was already taking countermeasures before the attacking technique could be perfected.

Group attacks were devastating once U-boats reached strike positions, but too many failed to make contact with convoys in the first place. This had not mattered so much during the previous autumn as an abundance of ships sailing independently of convoys ensured that each boat still achieved considerable success. By February 1941, lone sailings were becoming rarer and convoys noticeably harder to find. In addition to this, Britain had made a concerted effort to prevent ships falling behind convoys and becoming lone stragglers. Dönitz responded by emphasising, once again, the need for more boats, and the need to streamline both production and repair facilities in order to increase the time that each boat could spend at sea. About one and a half years were required to build a Type VIIC, plus a further six months for fitting out and training, and this meant that there were no prospects of any

A number of merchantmen were used to supply U-boats and to provide crews with slightly more roomy facilities. This photograph, taken near Narvik in Norway, shows the supply ship Tanger *with U-boats alongside.*

substantial increases in numbers for some time to come. So, in the hope of overcoming the problem of finding convoys, Dönitz made another attempt to obtain his own reconnaissance aircraft.

Using aircraft in this vital role had been considered long before the war, but an effective naval air arm with long-range aircraft had never been developed despite prewar exercises having shown that they would play an important role in any future conflict. Aircraft, like U-boats, had been prohibited under the terms of the Versailles Dictate and had only been under serious, open development for four and a half years by the time the war started. So in 1939, German naval flying was still in its infancy and when the fighting started, the few naval squadrons already established passed into Luftwaffe control. It was not until December 1940 that Grand Admiral Erich Raeder asked for their return. At the same time he suggested that special torpedo-carrying aircraft be built and long-range reconnaissance bombers be made available for naval work.

Hitler's decision to attach Bomber Squadron I/KG40 (The First Group of Kampfgeschwader 40) to the U-boat Command, while the Supreme Commander-in-Chief of the Luftwaffe (Reichsmarschall Hermann Göring) was absent on a hunting expedition, is well known today. So is Göring's subsequent journey to Lorient to request the return of the aircraft. Dönitz did not allow himself be intimidated by the Reichsmarschall and the two did not part amicably. Dönitz agreed to a Luftwaffe officer being given the job of liaising between the U-boat Command and the aircrews but the Luftwaffe continued to be difficult by preventing Dönitz from establishing a base at the airfield in Stavanger. Too many obstacles were put in the way of establishing a branch office for the U-boat Command in which trained naval officers could evaluate vital information the moment it arrived. Instead, the Luftwaffe appointed OL Martin Harlinghausen as Fliegerführer Atlantik (Air

Keroman U-boat bunkers under construction at Lorient.

Commander Atlantic), who started his military career as a naval officer and got on quite well with the U-boat men.

This was the first time that long-range aircraft had worked with submarines and when I/KG40 became operational on 7 January 1941, Dönitz was under no illusions as to the likely results. Despite his low expectations, it was rather disappointing that I/KG40 did not make contact with a single convoy during January, although the month ended on a positive note. On the twenty-sixth, U107 (KK Günter Hessler) proved that it was possible to home in on the radio beacon transmitted from an aircraft. The next significant success came on 9 February when U37 (KL Nicolai Clausen) directed aircraft onto the homeward bound convoy HG53. This reversal of roles has often been quoted as an example of poor navigation by aircrews, but it was, in fact, part of Dönitz's plans. U37 ran into the convoy during the late hours of the eighth, while on her way to West African waters. Following standing orders, Clausen took the role of shadow. Shortly after his report, the B-Dienst de-coded a British message suggesting that U37 had been sighted and it was this which prompted Dönitz to surprise the enemy by sending planes instead of a wolf pack. U37 was ordered to stick with the convoy, while five planes were made ready. Four of them managed to sink nine ships, and thus proved the benefits of co-operation between aircraft and submarines. Mechanical damage forced the fifth aircraft to make an emergency landing in Spain. During the night, before the arrival of the aircraft, Clausen had gone in for two attacks but once I/KG40 was on the way he acted only as director to home the aircraft onto their target. The following day, 10 February, Clausen received permission to attack again but by then he had lost contact. U37 found the convoy again, lost it and then located it again. Later, the heavy cruiser *Admiral Hipper* appeared on the scene, but further attacks by the U-boat were frustrated by nine unexplained torpedo failures.

U37's action against convoy HG53 was followed towards the end of February 1941 by the greatest single success of this type of action. It happened less than two weeks later when U47 (KL Günter Prien) directed aircraft to convoy OB290. U97 (KL Udo Heilmann) took over the shadowing task after U47 lost contact. Aircraft were again employed for an attack because surprise was thought to be on their side and no one from the small U-boat patrol line could get within range to attack. The attack resulted in the scattering of the convoy.

U959 (commissioned by OL Martin Duppel and later commanded by OL Friedrich Weitz) approaching the Dora II *U-boat bunker in Trondheim.*

A drydock section of the incomplete Dora II *bunker in Trondheim, photographed by Knut Sivertsen during the spring of 1985.*

These successes were short-lived, and by March there was considerable concern regarding the employment of aircraft, which is expanded upon in the next chapter. The main problem was on the acute shortage of aircraft. Kampfgeschwader 40 (I/KG40) or Squadron 40 sounds impressive, but the reality was that usually only two, sometimes three, aircraft were on patrol each day. Dönitz calculated that a minimum of twelve were required to cover the areas where convoys were expected. Air reconnaissance for U-boats remained low key, and as successes dwindled throughout the year the very concept of air support became a joke throughout the U-boat Arm.

The difficulties created by the introduction of aircraft represented only one of the problems experienced during that winter. Worse was the realisation that torpedoes were still not working properly. This came to light after several commanders reported a high number of merchantmen struggling behind convoys after attacks, and U-boat Command concluded that the ships had probably been hit but that the defective torpedoes had not been able to sink them. This problem had not arisen before simply because the convoy battles of the previous autumn had been too hectic to allow ships to be kept under observation after torpedoes had been fired. Furthermore, it is reasonable to suppose that men simply did not draw attention to ships they did not sink.

At first, in the summer of 1940, when the first failure reports appeared, the U-boat Command was not unduly perturbed, thinking that men were bound to make a few mistakes in the heat of battle. In September 1940, however, Günter Prien (U47) drew

Trondheim harbour photographed by Knut Sivertsen during the spring of 1985. The modified Dora II bunker can be seen in the background on the left and the incomplete Dora I on the right. The circular building in the foreground to the left is a brick personnel shelter.

Danzig in East Prussia during the winter 1941/42 with the liner Hamburg *being used as headquarters and accommodation ship for the 8th U-Flotilla.*

attention to a possible fault after he had seen one torpedo from a salvo of three break the surface of the water. Shortly after this, KK Erich Topp (U552) ran into St Nazaire after his first operational cruise as a U-boat commander with the news that only two ships had been sunk though fourteen torpedoes had been fired. Dönitz could not accept that these failures were simply the result of poor aiming; he was convinced that other factors lay behind them. Staff at the U-boat Command turned their attention to the log books and compiled an interesting list of incidents. And all the while, further reports, like the one concerning nine duds from U37, kept coming in. U-boat Command had to conclude that defective torpedoes were at the root of the problem, but this was hard to swallow, especially after all the effort made to eradicate the faults after the first winter of the war.

Dönitz at first shrugged off the incidents by suggesting a few possible causes such as the hardening of the oil as a result of cold weather, and he expected quick and easy solutions from the Torpedo Inspectorate.

Another frustration during this period of the war was caused by allied attacks on U-boats close to their home ports. The German navy was unable to provide satisfactory escort in the dangerous

Generalbaumeister Todt, who was responsible for building the concrete U-boat shelters, and Dönitz. Between them is KK Herbert Sohler, chief of the 7th U-Flotilla who earlier commanded U46.

waters off the German Bight and in the approaches to the Baltic and so progress was extremely difficult, as the U-boats, faced with the dangers of mines and aircraft, had to remain submerged during daylight, making progress in and out of Germany painfully slow. At times, boats were even held up in ports for short periods because the risks of running out were too high.

The number of British submarine excursions to the French Atlantic coast, however, had declined, probably because the winter weather was too rough for coastal deployment there, but the Royal Air Force had shown no signs of any letting up. Bomb aiming, however, was poor and the attacks devastated French buildings while inflicting little damage on German naval forces nearby. Dönitz felt certain, however, that both the intensity and success of the attacks would improve and he could see U-boats being destroyed at their repair berths. For this reason, Reichsminister Dr Fritz Todt visited Lorient on 10 March 1941 to discuss the construction of concrete shelters. This was not a new idea, since roofed protection had been provided during World War I and the bunker on Heligoland had already been completed. It did not take long for plans to go ahead for the construction to begin in La Pallice, St Nazaire, Brest, Bergen and Trondheim.

5. The Tide Turns

On 12 February 1941 Dönitz remarked, 'KL Herbert Kuppisch (U94), one of the old guard who joined the navy in 1933 before the re-introduction of national conscription, has only managed to sink three ships during a four-week spell in the once lucrative Rockall Bank area. These unsatisfactory results cannot be blamed on bad weather, poor visibility and long hours of darkness'. The suspicion that Britain was routing merchant traffic around the wolf packs made it necessary to spread patrol lines over larger areas. Since ships could only move northwards, the next pack was to be spread from the Hebrides to Iceland, though this meant leaving the southern approaches of North Channel clear of U-boats. It was hoped to close this gap with Italian boats later.

The first sign of a break in the winter stalemate came a week later on 19 February when a Condor, flying from France to Trondheim, reported having sunk two ships from convoy OB287 in square AM3443. Five U-boats were ordered into a patrol formation, while three Italian submarines were directed to its southern flank with a view of lengthening the short line. Visibility was reasonable, making it possible to leave a gap of 25 miles between each boat. Starting before first light on the twentieth, aircraft, flying at one- to two-hourly intervals, were dispatched for a co-ordinated search. Shortly before mid-day, the first of these sent a sighting report and the U-boats were immediately ordered to converge on the spot. The second aircraft, however, following at 1400 hours, reported quite different details. The convoy had either made a drastic change of course or there were two different groups of merchant ships at sea. If there was only one convoy, then the 1400 hours data meant the merchant ships would miss the pack. Assuming that the details from the morning sighting were correct, Dönitz ordered the patrol line to draw tighter together without regard to the Italians, on whom it was felt no one could rely. Then, to add to this confusion, a B-Dienst (Radio Monitoring Service) report of intercepted messages from attacked merchant ships suggested that the convoy was in a different location to the two positions given by the aircraft. Dönitz remarked that all the details appeared to be somewhat misleading and wondered whether Britain had introduced a special code for nautical positions, so that numbers could not be taken at their face value.

This unsuccessful hunt for convoy OB287 caused the U-boat Command to make the following points:

1   The U-boats were ordered to converge on a position given by aircraft during the late morning of the twentieth and it might have been better to have kept the patrol line sweeping a larger area until the convoy was sighted by a U-boat.

2   The weather could have impaired visibility for both the boats and the aircraft.

3   Boats' navigation could have been at fault.

4   Dönitz was to go to I/KG40 to obtain an accurate picture of the airmen's navigation abilities.

5   An effort was to be made to determine the accuracy of the positions given by the B-Dienst.

These views were modified a week later, following U96's (KL

KL Heinrich Lehmann-Willenbrock of U96 in the central control room, at the navigation periscope.

Heinrich Lehmann-Willenbrock) return to port. Details of the aircraft's bearings, recorded in the log, suggested that the position of the second sighting, the one of the afternoon, was correct and this led Dönitz to draw the following conclusions:

1   Considerable variations in positions given by aircraft had to be taken into account.

2   It was impossible to operate wolf packs on the sightings reported by I/KG40 and the searches had to continue until a convoy was sighted by a U-boat.

3   The best way to determine the accuracy of positions reported by I/KG40 was for as many U-boats as possible to take bearings on beacon signals from the planes.

The next opportunity to put these ideas into practice came on 3 March, after an aircraft had sighted another west-bound convoy, this time OB292. Once again U-boats returned empty handed, although the distance between the U-boat patrol line and the merchant ships was thought to have been too short for the convoy to escape. Apparently, the U-boats had been foiled by one of their own radio signals which had given away the position of the patrol line. It is not clear whether the source was detected by direction finders or whether the British had a lucky hit in deciphering the signal. In any event, the signal had come from U95 (KL Gerd Schreiber), which had used its radio from the middle of the patrol line to report that all its torpedoes had been expended. During the *post mortem* discussion, the U-boat Command again blamed failure on navigational mistakes and made the following points:

1   The accuracy of positions reported by aircraft was not good enough. An error of 70 nautical miles (130 km), as had been determined by U96's direction finder (KL Heinrich Lehmann-Willenbrock) had always to be taken into account. It seems highly likely that positions given by British radio and intercepted by the B-Dienst were correct.

2   Since it was only possible to keep one aircraft in the air at a time, it had to be assumed that the enemy's course was maintained only for the benefit of our observers, and might later change.

A new method of co-operation between aircraft and U-boats had to be found, although Dönitz felt that the problems could best be solved by simply having more aircraft. The following instructions were given to the commander of I/KG40:

1   At least two planes were to be in the air each day for the sole purpose of finding convoys. If possible, one was to fly after the other on the same course with a time gap of one to two hours.

From left to right: Erich Topp (U552), Claus Korth (U93), Engelbert Endrass (U46) and Herbert Kuppisch (U94) wearing the white summer uniform. Note that the national eagles on the right breast were made of metal for easy removal during cleaning.

2   On sighting a convoy, the course, position and speed were to be transmitted at once and this was to be followed by a good saturation of radio beacon signals. The composition of the convoy, as well as details of the escorts was to be radioed later. Aircraft were to remain in contact with the convoy as long as fuel allowed.

3   The second plane was to aim at the convoy reported by the first and, on sighting it, make its own report from its own navigational notes, without reference to any details given by the first plane.

4   A previous order, to keep the enemy under surveillance without attacking, given shortly after the failure with convoy OB287, was rescinded and aircraft were again given permission to attack. The U-boat Command wanted to encourage merchant ships to reveal their positions by sending distress signals.

(Many books give the impression that reconnaissance aircraft flew on reciprocal courses, with one starting in France and the other in Norway. Dönitz's diary at this point makes it quite clear that planes flew on similar courses, one behind the other.)

Two other convoy attacks were significant during this period, although the importance of the events was not realised by the U-boat Command until much later. On 6 March 1941, KL Günter Prien (U47) sighted Convoy OB293 towards the north of the new operations area and called in U70 (KL Joachim Matz) as well as U99 (KL Otto Kretschmer). U47, however, was over confident, approached too close and was forced under for a brief period. Two days later, a repeat performance of over confidence appears to have cost U47 its life. It was sunk by the destroyer *Wolverine* while shadowing the convoy. U70 had been sunk only a few hours earlier, as a result of an attack by the corvettes *Camellia* and *Arbutus*. The details of these atacks have been previously unclear. However, Joachim Matz and some of his crew survived to be rescued, and the details given above are based on the latest research by the German U-boat Archive. The exact details are insignificant as far as the convoy war was concerned and the important point is that two boats went down in what was virtually one attack. What is more, another U-boat might nearly have been sunk as well. UA (KK Hans Eckermann), built as *Batiray* for Turkey and commissioned into the German Navy as U-Ausland (U-Abroad), was seriously damaged during an attack on 7 March, when torpedo failures brought swift retaliation from escorts. As a result, Eckermann started limping to France, instead of joining Prien and Matz. The final result of the battle for convoy OB293 was seven ships and two U-boats sunk, plus UA seriously damaged. All but one boat was repulsed and only the experienced U99 (KL Otto Kretschmer) managed to get within shooting range without too much harassment. U99 probably slipped past the escorts while they were attending to other attackers. This was the first time that U-boats had met with serious opposition and the incident played a significant part in the reversal of their role from hunters to hunted.

The next important incident took place shortly after mid-day of 15 March, when U110 (KL Fritz-Julius Lemp) sighted the 41 ships of the eastward-bound convoy, HX112. The 5th Escort Group, under Commander Donald Macintyre, had received useful instruction in combating U-boats and the ships were carrying a new baby: operational radar, known as Type 286 Radar. The merchantmen ran into the U-boat patrol line but, unlike the previous autumn, now many of the approaching boats were driven off and only a few of the more experienced commanders managed to take advantage of the attention being given to their colleagues and creep in close enough to attack. U100 (KL Joachim Schepke) was unfortunate to be detected by *Vanoc*'s (Commander Donald Macintyre) radar, and was rammed and sunk. Only the few men on the conning tower were fortunate enough to survive by jumping clear.

Meanwhile, U99, having expended all her torpedoes, had withdrawn to take over the shadowing task. The details of her fate have been recorded by her commander, Flottillenadmiral Federal German Navy Otto Kretschmer, in a letter written in 1977, as follows:

Commissioning U21 (KL Fritz Frauenheim) on 3 August 1936. U33, in the background, was commissioned just a fortnight earlier by Ottoheinrich Junker. U21 was a small coastal boat of Type IIB and U33, a Type VIIA, the forerunner of the most important Atlantic boat (Type VIIC). The photograph was taken at the Blücher Bridge in Kiel and shows the prewar white conning towers.

There were no rules regarding behaviour when approached by a destroyer. [The Germans often referred to escorts as destroyers.] Obviously, the commander knew that he had to remain undetected to get into a shooting position, but how he did it was entirely up to him. At night, once escorts came too close, he was free to dive or to show the approaching enemy the smallest silhouette and run away. Before the war, the underwater approach was recommended and as time went on we learned it was easier than anticipated to approach the enemy. It was only a case of nerves. At night, I always tried to break through the escorts on the surface and then shoot from within the ranks of the convoy, rather than from the recommended range of a kilometre or so. The enemy was bound to search around the convoy, not inside it. So far, Dönitz had only advocated the wolf pack technique, but he had not told anyone how to face the enemy. Instead, he informed new commanders about latest developments and left them to work out their own plans.

Every commander could make his own rules regarding behaviour of his boat and I had given the following orders:

1   Aircraft in sight: dive at once.
2   Merchant ship in sight: remain at extreme limit of visibility.

3   Destroyer in sight, but still behind the horizon: call commander to bridge.

4   Destroyer in sight at night: run away showing the smallest possible sihouette and call commander to bridge.

The decisive point in these decisions was the fact that U-boats became virtually stationary once they were below the surface and could easily be located by Asdic. There was no way in which our early torpedoes could hit destroyers and it did not take long for the enemy to realise this. Our only chance of survival was to run away.

Despite considerable leaks caused by depth charges from HMS *Walker*, U99 returned briefly to the surface before sinking. A few minutes earlier, the duty officer on the top of the conning tower (Kretschmer was down below) had ordered 'Alarm', realising that a lookout's negligence had put U99 into a desperate situation by allowing Donald Macintyre's destroyer to approach too close.

I should like to emphasise that the escorts' primary role was the protection of the convoy and they were not allowed to remain away from it for any length of time, even to hunt a U-boat. This changed once escorts were available in larger numbers. Support groups were then formed to remain behind to kill the U-boat or keep it under water until it had used all its electricity and could only surface and scuttle. This is one reason why people like Captain Walker RN, with their sloops of the Starling class, could achieve such a high rate of sinkings. Escort commanders, like Donald Macintyre, found it far more difficult to sink U-boats.

After the battle for convoy HX112 in southern Icelandic waters, a period of inactivity set in in those northern areas while the southern reaches, off Rockall Bank, appeared to be carrying more traffic. This pattern, having been deduced from information gathered by passing U-boats as well as by German aircraft, seemed to represent a new turn of events. During the previous autumn, convoys were running along fixed tracks and continued to sail into wolf packs, even though another convoy, only a short distance ahead, might have suffered heavy losses. In March 1941, the transatlantic routes seemed to become more flexible, with convoys taking positive action to avoid patrol lines. This, as well as the heavy losses of U-boats in Icelandic waters, caused Dönitz to evacuate the northern reaches of the operations area towards the

*U73, a Type VIIB under KL
Helmut Rosenbaum, leaving
Lorient for the Mediterranean.*

end of March 1941. The move further west was not of the U-boat
Command's own free will but was dictated by the need to avoid
escorts and aircraft. For the first time since the start of the war,
patrol lines were ordered west of 25° West.

On returning to port, commanders brought a different picture
than that which had been envisaged by the U-boat Command. The
latter assumed an increase in the number of escorts and the introduction of a new type of weapon. The crews, on the other hand, had
noticed nothing new in the enemy procedure since the summer of
the previous year. Dönitz's decision to evacuate the operations area
seemed, therefore, a bad one and one not based on reason and,
indeed, by mid April U-boats were returning to eastern waters,
where they had better chances of finding and fighting convoys.
Dönitz remarked that the heavy losses of March had to be accepted
as the new norm, and that Britain was doing well in locating
U-boats; furthermore, that the small numbers of U-boats at sea
meant that it was becoming easier for convoys to avoid them.

Historians looking for the turning point of the U-boat war would
do well to analyse the events of this period in detail. It marks a
drastic change in the war at sea from which U-boats never recovered. There only followed pyrrhic victories for U-boats, but this
has not yet been fully realised.

6. Radio or Treason?

The reduction in sunk tonnage during April 1941 led Dönitz to believe that there was a temporary lull in enemy merchant traffic. This was supported neither by the Supreme Naval Command's research nor by the intensity of radio messages intercepted by the B-Dienst. The Naval War Staff suggested that there appeared to be a systematic avoidance of U-boat patrol lines and, once more, there came the question, 'How does Britain know about U-boat dispositions?' Dönitz's long-standing suspicion that the radio codes were being broken by the British had led him, on several occasions, to approach experts at the Supreme Naval Command to check whether there could be a leak in this quarter. Each time he was told the same story: that the complexity of the coding machine made any break into the system impossible. It was agreed that it might be feasible for an outsider to read a few messages shortly after capturing a machine set with the code for a day, but after 24 hours the change in the code system rendered a seized machine useless. Every time Dönitz approached the Naval Command experts gave good reasons why even the consideration of a break into the code was sheer folly and the U-boat Command was thus satisfied that this part of its operations was safe. On the other hand, the German B-Dienst was able to read British signals with ease and for a long time provided a key service for directing wolf packs.

Already before the war, German messages were set into code by a machine known as Enigma. This had been universally adopted by all German Armed Forces and several branches produced their own specialised versions. The navy's machine, known as Schlüsselmaschine M (Code Writer M; The German Navy called itself Marine more often than Kriegsmarine, whence the M), consisted of a typewriter keyboard with several wheels which jumbled the depressed letters electrically. At first there were slots for three wheels and later for four. There was a choice of a number of different wheels to be slotted in and, on top of this, several wires had to be plugged into the base. Wheels were swopped around daily, the starting position of each varied and the wiring added even more complexity. There were several different cypher systems, which meant that one branch of the navy could not interpret messages sent

The author experimenting with a naval Enigma code writer at the German U-boat Archive. The picture in the background is of the World War I U-boat Ace, Otto Hersing.

One of the early Enigma code writers. The 26 sockets at the front had to connected according to the pattern of the day. Next, the three (and later four) wheels at the top had to be inserted in the appropriate order and the correct starting position of each adjusted. Then the message was typed on the keyboard and the coded letter was illuminated between the keyboard and the three wheels. The switch at the top right is for on, off and battery test. A dark green piece of plastic was placed over the letters to prevent the light shining out at night.

U172 with doubled sun sector air lookouts. German binoculars were not fitted with special filters. Instead, each boat carried a number of different types of sun glasses for use against a variety of conditions and the binoculars butted neatly onto these.

for another. Some signals were also coded more than once. For example, the radio operator might end up with a coded message headed 'Officer Only'. An officer, then using his code settings, would pass the text through the machine for a second time. He might end up with readable text or more jumbled letters labelled 'Commander Only'.

The story of how Britain managed to break into the German code is well known today, but it must be emphasised that this was not known to the U-boat Command nor anyone else on the German side. In fact, this brilliant exploit was hardly known in Britain, and during the war remained one of the best kept secrets. Only a handful of men in the Royal Navy knew it was being done and great care was taken to give the impression that the information came from other sources. The secrecy surrounding Enigma was not lifted until 1972 and even then Dönitz found it hard to believe. The idea that Britain was breaking the naval codes certainly did not feature a great deal in German wartime thinking.

In April 1941, the U-boat Command introduced further restrictions in the use of radio and the Naval War Staff appointed a Radio Intelligence Officer to Dönitz's headquarters, who was responsible for analysing enemy radio traffic, with the view to looking for possible clues as to how Britain located U-boats at sea.

Britain's prewar expenditure of considerable resources into radio detection techniques was well known by German Intelligence and information recovered aboard HM submarine *Seal* (LtCdr R P Lonsdale), captured in May 1940 as well as material found in French bases, suggested that Britain had made considerable progress in this field. It was also assumed that more direction finding stations had been set up after the loss of co-operation from French establishments. Earlier during the war, when the threat of Britain being able to detect the sources of radio signals was first realised, the Germans found that errors of at least 70 nautical miles (130 km) were made and in many cases these extended to 500 nautical miles; the U-boat Command was thus not greatly concerned. By early 1941, however, the B-Dienst produced the most disturbing evidence to suggest that Britain had located the two weather boats, U123 (KL Karl-Heinz Moehle) and U96 (KL Heinrich Lehmann-Willenbrock). Dönitz pointed out that both de-coded positions were somewhat wide of the mark, but nevertheless, it appeared as if Britain could now pin-point the sources of short signals, whose duration had been considered too brief for direction finders. It is interesting to add here that for 14 days during this period the two weather boats represented 50 percent of the total numbers at sea.

Experts, appointed to look into the problem of this detection, came to the conclusion that Britain probably could locate the sources of some radio messages, but that for the most part targets were detected visually, following an analysis of tactical and navigational data. These experts concluded on a rather defeatist note: 'It is impossible to say how the enemy discovered or reacted to radio messages'. And they made the big mistake of over-estimating the strength of anti-U-boat forces in the Atlantic, stating that, 'There is a great deal of enemy activity and sooner or later something will be bound to run into U-boats'.

Early in June 1941, the following new radio procedures were introduced as a stop-gap measure until the situation could be clarified.

1   *Travelling to or from operations area:* Messages should be kept to a minimum and radio not used if it could put other boats into jeopardy.

2   *In operations areas:* Radio only to be used: a, when the boat's position is definitely know to the enemy; b, on instructions from the U-boat Command; c, for important tactical information.

3   To make tracking more difficult until new procedures are introduced, radio wavelength should be changed frequently.

4   *The following are included as important tactical reasons for using the radio:* Enemy sightings, weather reports, information about quantities of fuel, start of a homeward bound voyage, and entering or leaving the Bay of Biscay. (Previously, boats had sent a message when they approached 10° West; this was altered to 15° West once British aircraft started to play a greater role.)

Obersteuermann (Navigator) of U172 shooting the mid-day sun. Navigation became quite a problem, especially towards the end of the war, when boats were forced under for long periods and could surface only briefly under cloudy skies.

It is interesting to note that these new instructions did not make the radio logs any thinner and it appears as if there followed no significant reduction in radio traffic. Perhaps this was due to the great increase in young commanders who were largely untrained and not brought up in terror of being detected through their radios. Many of the older men could quote unfortunate victims of both wars, who were sunk shortly after having broadcast. To a certain extent, the restrictions in the use of radio were self defeating. The rapid change in frequencies probably resulted in many messages not reaching their destinations and the number of repeat messages increased.

During this radio code enquiry, Dönitz conducted another thorough spy hunt throughout U-boat headquarters and took steps to prevent unauthorised access to U-boat dispositions. This involved

U172 under KL Carl Emmermann (in the middle, wearing white hat). On the left are the special binoculars clipped on top of the torpedo aimer. Bearings from the device were automatically transmitted down below.

all nautical data such as speeds, directions and positions being specially coded to make it impossible for an outsider to read numbers from positions marked on command charts. The practice of sending U-boat dispositions to the German liaison officer for Italian submarines, to the Commander for Aircraft in the Atlantic, as well as several other associated offices was stopped. The Supreme Naval Command was asked to prohibit unauthorised listening to U-boat wavelengths and to reduce the legal listeners to an absolute minimum. In retrospect, it is a little difficult to understand the arguments behind this request. Did the U-boat Command think a naval radio station was listening to U-boat broadcasts and then passing the information on to the enemy? Would such a radio spy not locate himself out of reach of German security forces?

The Supreme Naval Command and the Naval War Staff were still located at Tirpitzufer in Berlin, while Dönitz was a long distance away in Lorient, and it is sometimes difficult to determine how much information actually reached the right people in the German High Command. During the first week of May 1940, the Naval Command certainly received Dönitz's warnings about a possible breach of security. So it is a little difficult to explain, considering the real concern about spies from within and the Navy's reputation for being the most security conscious of the armed forces, why U-boat dispositions in the Atlantic were still being sent by land line to the U-boat Officer responsible for the Black Sea, to the German Admiral in the Balkans and to the German Naval Command in Italy. None of these had any need to know what U-boats were doing in the Atlantic.

7. More Frustrations and Disappointments

Reasonably accurate evaluation of the situation in the Atlantic was only possible after commanders returned for debriefing. Therefore, it was not until the end of April that the U-boat Command could obtain a detailed picture of the events in March, and the following points were recorded in the log during the first week of May 1941.

Enemy merchant traffic is spread over the whole of the Atlantic from Iceland to Porcupine Bank and only converges in the immediate approaches to North Channel or close to the Faeroes–Hebrides passage. There appears to be no traffic north of Iceland and the diverging of shipping across the Atlantic does not follow any particular pattern.

Anti-U-boat measures, both from ships and aircraft, are increasing noticeably in the present operations area. Longer hours of daylight are probably also helping to make our attacks significantly more difficult. U-boats still manage to sight convoys, but are frequently forced under, impeding their attacks or disrupting the shadowing process. Noteworthy successes will not be possible under such circumstances and we must resign ourselves to the fact that only occasional chance attacks will succeed. These will not be sufficient to achieve anything. Attempts to work with aircraft have been disappointing. There has been no success with aircraft directing U-boats to a convoy. Navigational errors appear to be the biggest problem, although the aircrafts' limited range and consequently the short time they can remain with convoys is also a contributing factor in their inefficiency.

It is interesting to note that during the following day an aircraft landed at 1530 hours to report a convoy which had been sighted at 0830 hours. After four months of reconnaissance flights, the Luftwaffe still made the most elementary in mistakes in not reporting shipping the moment it was spotted nor supporting their finds by sending a good saturation of radio beacon signals. Dönitz had already abandoned hopes of close co-operation and went on to say that, 'The bad experiences of the past weeks have shown that the U-boat Command must do without aircraft'.

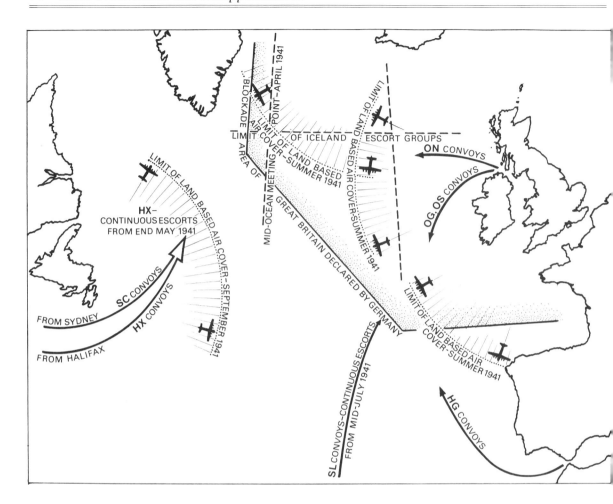

LIMIT OF LAND BASED AIR COVER—APRIL 1941

BLOCKADE AREA OF

LIMIT OF LAND BASED AIR COVER—SUMMER 1941

LIMIT OF ICELAND ESCORT GROUPS

ON CONVOYS

OG, OS CONVOYS

LIMIT OF LAND BASED AIR COVER—SEPTEMBER 1941

HX—
CONTINUOUS ESCORTS
FROM END MAY 1941

MID-OCEAN MEETING POINT—APRIL 1941

GREAT BRITAIN DECLARED BY GERMANY

SC CONVOYS

HX CONVOYS

FROM SYDNEY

FROM HALIFAX

SL CONVOYS—CONTINUOUS ESCORTS
FROM MID-JULY 1941

LIMIT OF LAND BASED AIR COVER—SUMMER 1941

HG CONVOYS

*British counter measures:
summer 1941.*

Italian U-boats in the Atlantic were considered in a similar vein, and Dönitz reckoned on little support from them. His diary states, 'Their officers have been given the opportunity of going through Baltic training establishments and they have been in action with German boats, but all to no avail. Their results are still unsatisfactory; they do not see anything, they report nothing, or only do so when it is too late; and their tactical skills can be rated as zero'. A few weeks later he refused for a second time to take command of Italian submarines in the Atlantic, saying, 'The superstructures of the boats are too massive for employment against convoys at night'. Dönitz's reason for not wanting to command Italian boats – to prevent the Italians having an excuse to take control of German units in the Mediterranean – has been mentioned earlier.

The report concluded with the remark, 'The U-boat Command must look to new ways for bringing success'. Heavy defences near enemy coasts made it impossible to continue operations in these once lucrative areas. The apparent shortage of convoy protection towards the west forced Dönitz to look at this potentially good area. The move brought several disadvantages. For example, it would result in longer passages, less time in operational areas and the spreading out of boats over larger areas which in turn would result in the inevitable loss of each boat's efficiency.

These observations reached the Naval War Staff by the third week of May 1941, just when the *Bismarck* was beginning its one and only sortie. Information from the U-boat Command did not automatically progress further and Hitler would only have been officially informed if Grand Admiral Erich Raeder had included the information in one of his regular situation reports or directed his representative to mention the matter. Some of the problems experienced by U-boat Command appear to have reached the Führer. On 25 July, after the loss of *Bismarck* had been digested and the war at sea re-assessed, Hitler referred to Dönitz's earlier worries by saying, 'There is no evidence for the fears expressed by the U-boat Command through the Grand Admiral'. This somewhat casual remark, dropped into a long speech, leads one to wonder whether he was actually in possession of the facts collected and presented by the U-boat Command. Looking back through the minutes of the proceedings between Raeder and Hitler, it is noticeable that the worries of the U-boat Command, expressed in this and the preceding chapter, do not appear to have featured.

Admiral Hans-Georg von Friedeburg (left), chief of the U-boat Arm's Organisation Department and KS Werner Hartmann, who had commanded U37 before becoming Flotilla Commander and then U-boat Flag Officer.

The beginning of *Bismarck*'s voyage brought an interesting insight into Hitler's knowledge of the Navy. A dinner aboard *Tirpitz* in Gotenhafen, after his inspection of *Bismarck*, gave him the opportunity to speak to naval officers. The Führer sat between the Fleet Commander, Admiral Günther Lütjens and the two battleship captains, Kpt. z. S Ernst Lindemann and Kpt. z. S Karl Topp. Erich Raeder, the Supreme Commander-in-Chief of the Navy, was absent. The assembled company of many invited Knights Cross (of the Iron Cross) holders was most impressed by Hitler's knowledge of naval matters. It seemed to be too comprehensive to challenge and despite him throwing a few questions to his audience, no one made an attempt to answer them. Afterwards, the two U-boat aces, Teddy and Gerd Suhren, discussed the events of the day. Both were impressed by the Führer, but Teddy could not help observing how Hitler had done all the talking all day. Although

This photograph is reputed to show the commissioning of U201. The man with the white cap is KK Adalbert Schnee and the insignia, the badge of the town of Remscheid, confirm that this is U201, but for a commissioning the men would have been better dressed. The beards and the dirty clothing suggest the boat has just come back to port. The two pockets above the navigation light were designed to hold a horseshoe-shaped lifebelt.

U71 (KL Walter Flachsenberg) with an unusual modification to the wind deflector at the top of the conning tower. The lip, halfway up the tower, was a spray deflector and the gun is of 88mm calibre.

Hitler demonstrated a wide textbook knowledge of naval matters, but, the brothers asked themselves, 'How can he know what is going on at the front if no one dares approach him?' Hitler talked about building more battleships in Norway and Teddy wanted to know when they would be ready. It seemed that they would take years to complete and this suggested that the war was going to last a long time.

The violations against German shipping in the Pan American Neutrality Zone, the sinking of the *Bismarck* and the sinking of all but one supply ship at sea during the early summer of 1941 influenced the German attitude in favour of U-boats. Raeder's attempts to convince Hitler of the potential of submarines became more forceful and frequent as the autumn wore on. On 15 Septem-

U565 (OL Johann Jebsen, who was killed in action in September 1944), a Type VIIC built at Blohm und Voss in Hamburg. The white tactical mark, next to the horseshoe-shaped lifebelt, was used for identification during trials and training. Twenty-nine Blohm und Voss boats carried this distinctive recognition mark, which was erased after completion of training.

ber, Raeder told him that action in the Atlantic against merchant shipping was the only sensible battle of the whole war and that three to four times the present number of U-boats was required. Raeder also suggested several ways of increasing the numbers at sea since production lines, already working to capacity, could not cope with an immediate increase.

A month later, the situation had deteriorated still further. Dönitz was fighting the all-important tonnage war with an average of five to ten boats at sea. At times they were either all going out or coming home leaving none available to make contact with the enemy. About twice this number of boats was employed by other naval authorities for alternative tasks, such as reporting weather, landing agents, escorting surface units, or cruising the Arctic seas in support of big ship operations. In the official history, *The War at Sea*, Stephen Roskill emphasises the extent to which the shortage of U-boats in the shipping lanes was a great advantage to Britain.

Although the setbacks seemed to dominate the U-boat war, there were successes. Earlier in February 1941, another sortie into the warmer waters of the South Atlantic had been attempted and on 2 July, Günter Hessler (U107) returned to Lorient from the most successful cruise of the whole war. He was married to Dönitz's daughter, Ursula, and like her two brothers, Klaus and Peter, received no favours from the Old Lion. Dönitz did not even apply for a Knights Cross for his son-in-law, and Grand Admiral Raeder sent a terse memorandum, saying he would award it personally if the Commander-in-Chief for U-boats failed to do so. As a result Hessler received the Knights Cross.

At times, Dönitz appears to have displayed a somewhat callous attitude towards others and it is possible that he used his ability of making quick decisions to flex his anger at the wrong people. Take U109 as an example. On 30 May 1941, KK Hans Georg Fischer returned to France at the end of his first voyage and was immediately relieved of his duty. Dönitz had only a brief chat with the other officers and justified his decision with the remark that Fischer had conducted himself in an unsettled manner. Training at the Agru Front had already produced doubts concerning his abilities and during a depth charge attack he had dived the boat too deep. Fischer's replacement, Ajax Bleichrodt, went out only once with U109 before asking for the incompetent engineering officer to be removed and this wish was carried out. No enquiry ever followed into what amounted to the sacking of a commander and Fischer had to live with the tarnished image for the rest of the war. Wolfgang Hirschfeld (U109's radio operator and later a historian) said the fault lay with other officers, not with Fischer. A few months later, there followed Dönitz's inexplicable reaction to U570's capture. On learning from the British press that the commander, KL Hans-Joachim Rahmlow, had suffered from gas poisoning, Dönitz concluded that the incident could be explained by the Commander being out of action and the First Officer, OL Berndt, handing the boat over to the enemy. The Supreme Naval Command objected most strongly to this half-page-long statement, saying that the first officer should not be burdened with guilt until it had been proved. At the same time, by offering an alternative theory based on vague foreign press reports, the admirals displayed the same stagnant attitude as Dönitz.

Most of the setbacks listed by Dönitz throughout 1941 were considered as temporary and there were great hopes of another successful period. This was made clear in the situation report sent to Hitler on 25 July, in which Dönitz's views about the prospects of the future concluded, 'Despite the poor results, one must look at this as a passing phase'. When looking at the overall war statistics, however, the picture seems far from gloomy and many historians have forgotten the difficulties and setbacks of 1941. The second generation of U-boat commanders, men like Adalbert Schnee, Teddy Suhren and Engelbert Endrass, who had learned their trade under the first great aces, produced some successes. But, although U-boat men fought harder than ever before, they also died quicker.

U43 (KL Wolfgang Lüth) with Martin Becker keeping lookout from an improvised platform attached to the sky or navigation periscope. The white circle on the conning tower was made by a paper hole punch and it is not part of the structure.

8. Wolf Packs Try to Bite

Dönitz's fundamental objective of only employing U-boats against merchant shipping and concentrating them in limited patrol lines led him into conflict with the Navy War Staff which wanted to disperse boats over larger areas and use them for a wider variety of roles such as supply ships and weather boats. The bad weather of the 1940-41 winter had decided Dönitz against sending his forces further away into the South Atlantic, but feasibility studies, carried out by the Supreme Naval Command before the war, led to plans for submarines to go south with the first wave of auxiliary cruisers heading towards the Indian ocean and the Pacific. Dönitz strongly resisted pressures to attempt such undertakings, and in the early stages of the war few U-boats actually sailed south, even though a number of auxiliary cruisers carried stores and provisions for U-boats.

The deplorable results in the North Atlantic during the spring of 1941, however, coincided with Dönitz's realisation that one U-boat which had achieved next to nothing in the South Atlantic, U65 (KK Hans-Gerrit von Stockhausen), had been located in the wrong area off Africa. These factors, combined with the completion of larger numbers of long-distance boats of Type IX, caused him to change his views and plans were formulated for simultaneous operations in both the North and South Atlantic. It was intended that a group of U-boats would operate with the support of a surface supply ship. These latter vessels were hastily converted merchant ships. The small number of fast, purpose-built supply ships were required by surface units and could only be used by U-boats as long as there was no interference with Naval Command plans.

In the north, North Channel had been evacuated as a result of heavy losses during March. U-boats had moved west of 20° West but by the middle of April they were back, and this brought immediate success when convoy SC26 ran into a wolf pack on 1 April and lost some 12 ships, even before all U-boats could be positioned in the formation. Successes, however, were shortlived, for at this point in the war the British made a major breakthrough into the German secret code, something which the German experts declared as impossible. The story is well known today. It started before the war with a reconstructed German cypher machine being

brought from Poland to London and it continued with the concerted efforts made to capture more parts of the device. Attempts by
cryptoanalysts at Bletchley Park in Buckinghamshire to understand
German messages were given an unexpected boost on 9 May 1941,
when U110 (KL Fritz-Julius Lemp) fell into British hands. No one
on the German side, not even the survivors of U110, knew that their
boat had been captured. From this boat, Britain gained a coding
machine, together with notes to operate it for five or more weeks.
The Royal Navy Operational Intelligence Centre in London utilised
this special intelligence to the very best advantage by sinking nine
supply ships in June 1941. The timing of this capture could not have
been better. It was just a few weeks before the first and only cruise of
the *Bismarck*, when more than ten supply ships were positioned in
isolated locations around the Atlantic. Nine of them vanished in
one well co-ordinated operation which left their dependents with
dire problems. In addition, all U-boat operations in the South
Atlantic and western side of the North Atlantic were put at risk. It is
interesting to note that Britain never managed to break into the
code used by German auxiliary cruisers, though the few operating
in the South Atlantic were put at risk through the U-boat code being

*KL Heino Bohmann (killed in
action on 12 September 1942)
of U88 stepping ashore. Before
the war, the white version of the
blue naval cap was frequently
worn by U-boat men but later it
became a custom for only
commanders to wear white hats
on U-boats. There were no
rules about who could wear
white hats on U-boats. It was
just a fad which evolved.*

Southern waters: 1941.

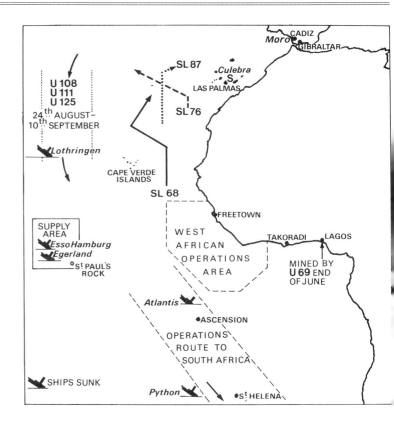

broken. They either transmitted by means of the U-boat code in order to refuel them or broadcast their positions to U-boats to prevent the latter from sinking their own ships.

Knowledge of the events at sea trickled back to Germany only slowly and several weeks passed before the seriousness of the situation was realised. First, an Italian submarine reported the presence of an aircraft carrier near the Cape Verde Islands, and Dönitz, to his annoyance, had to order meetings with supply ships to take place only during the hours of darkness. Four weeks later, U93 (KL Claus Korth), with 50 survivors on board, reported the sinking of the supply ship *Belchen* off Greenland. Dönitz ordered the survivors to be put aboard another supply ship so that U93 could continue its mission but Korth was most unhappy with this, reckoning that such deviation would cost too much fuel and put everybody's life in jeopardy if U93 failed to find the second ship. As a result of ignoring Dönitz's order, and instead making for France, Korth unwittingly revealed the dangers of broadcasting. Crawling

Claus Korth of U93 with his Obersteuermann and Watch Officer, Bruno Barber, who later became commander of U58, U220 and was killed in action in October 1943.

home, trying to avoid trouble, U93 was overtaken by a convoy. Korth decided against broadcasting and shadowing it because he thought such action would reveal his position; and he thought that his over full boat would be unable to withstand a depth charge attack. Dönitz thought that this was a mistaken decision and later reprimanded Korth, saying, 'There were boats all over the Atlantic looking for convoys while you were sitting quietly under the biggest. You should at least have broadcast its position'. In his anger, Dönitz failed to notice why Korth had managed something which had eluded every other U-boat. The convoy ran into U93 for the simple reason that Korth had deviated from the broadcast plan and the British were thus unaware of his position. This was by no means an isolated case. Several other boats found themselves in similar circumstances, making contact with allied shipping after some misfortune caused them to act independently of plans broadcast by U-boat Command. One wonders whether a naval intelligence department, analysing such incidents, might have deduced that U-boats whose positions had not been broadcast seemed to run into convoys.

The news of the sinking of the *Belchen* had hardly been digested before U38 (KL Heinrich Liebe) reported that the tanker *Egerland* could not be found. The news from U93 had been irritating enough for Dönitz but this incident was far more serious as there were a number of U-boats which were totally dependent on *Egerland*. Her

Adalbert Schnee wearing a sheepskin coat and using a megaphone to shout orders for docking. The binoculars are standard Zeiss naval issue 7 × 50 glasses.

loss put the entire South Atlantic operations at risk and forced the recall of all boats from African waters. *Egerland* had been sent out to supply auxiliary cruisers, and these raider activities were curtailed as well.

South Atlantic operations were limited to the African side of the ocean to avoid the Pan American Neutrality Zone, which had been declared by the United States shortly after the outbreak of the war. Since Hitler wished to avoid giving the Americans an excuse for joining the war, he had ordered western regions to be avoided. But, as Dönitz complained to the Supreme Naval Command on the several occasions, 'the term "neutrality" is heavily weighed against Germany, as United States warships permit British ships to seek shelter in the area'. Made aware of the problem, Grand Admiral Raeder approached Hitler for permission to enter the western Atlantic, but this was refused.

Towards the end of June 1941, Dönitz dictated his thoughts about the recent trends in the Atlantic as follows, 'Our set-up at sea has not produced the expected results. I had hoped to have put patrol lines at traffic junctions, yet there appear to be several reasons why enemy shipping has not been caught. Fog, ice and poor weather appear to be contributing factors, but shipping is probably penetrating patrol lines without being seen or it is travelling in the German shipping routes, where we cannot attack. [This so-called Prize Route was established as a safe passage for ships captured by surface raiders to run into France]. It is also possible that enemy ships are breaking through patrol lines during poor visibility, possibly with the aid of long-range detection equipment (radar)'.

The pages of the U-boat Command diary for June and July are dominated by reports of torpedo failure but Dönitz makes no comment about these. Instead, two weeks later, he returns to the old problem of the U-boats' inability to locate convoys and makes the point that this can only be solved by having more eyes at sea.

During this troubled period there was a significant episode in the history of submarine warfare. For the first time since aircraft were used for reconnaissance, they managed to track a convoy and successfully guide U-boats to the scene. The operation began on 24 July, after the B-Dienst detected the presence of convoys OG69 and SL80. Eight boats were directed towards OG69 and six towards the other group. Both convoys were sighted and every participating boat managed to take a bearing on the radio beacon from the aircraft. Furthermore, the positions and course details reported by I/KG40 tallied with data from B-Dienst. The hunt for SL80 was

U371 (KL Heinrich Driver) coming into port. Behind him are Engineering Officer OL Günther, First Watch Officer Kurt Petersen, who later became commander of U541, and Second Watch Officer Otto Weber, who became commander of U709. The commander's pennant and a pennant denoting one ship sunk are flying from the commander's flag staff. In the front is the raised rod aerial and on the right the partly extended attack periscope.

called off during the night, after contact with it was lost, but the chase with OG69 continued and seven ships were sunk on 27-28 July. Dönitz was pleased with the limited success for it represented the first time that aircraft had guided U-boats to a convoy. Most of the U-boat commanders in the wolf pack were young and inexperienced and for the whole of the operation the U-boat Command kept the situation under control, constantly sending advice. Dönitz remarked that this was vital since the new commanders' three weeks of tactical training had not allowed them to learn all the things which had earlier been imparted over several years. The U-boat Command's report concludes with the remark that once the enemy had been sighted, wolf pack techniques still worked. Finding convoys was the major obstacle to success and it was thought that this could only be solved by having more boats. For the future, the

U-boat Command looked forward to the introduction of new radar detection equipment aboard U-boats and new torpedoes.

With each succeeding month of the year, an ever increasing number of U-boats were forced under by British escorts, and during the summer months commanders started reporting more determination from their attackers. This new aspect of the war was not acknowledged in the U-boat Command's war diary, though it was quite apparent in many actions. For example, KL Philipp Schüler (U141) attacked the outward bound convoy OS1 off Northern Ireland shortly before the 5th Escort Group (Cdr Donald Macintyre) appeared and he found himself pushed under for a period of 24 hours during which he was harassed by constant depth charge bombardment. Previously, such attacks had only lasted for minutes, or occasionally for a few hours, but certainly never for a complete day.

One solution to this problem was for the boats in a wolf pack to attack simultaneously and so stretch the capacity of the escorts as to allow some U-boats to steal through the screen. Radar was thought to be only one of the factors contributing to the Royal Navy's greater successes. Reinhard Hardegen of U123 returned to port and reported how his men had sighted a Condor bomber of I/KG40 circling over what could have been a U-boat many miles away on the other side of the horizon, and thought that the enemy might be detecting the presence of U-boats in this way. Other commanders, returning towards the end of August 1941, told of what appeared to be a new form of convoy defence. They thought the merchant ships were now protected with two sets of escorts, one staying with the merchantmen as an inner ring, while another group travelled much further away, out of sight of the convoy. It was believed that this outer ring also shot star shells at night long distances from the convoys to draw U-boats away from their real targets.

At this juncture, as the second year of war drew to a close, Dönitz remarked, 'The increasing difficulty in shadowing convoys is made worse by the inexperience of the young commanders, who have slim prospects of keeping contact long enough for an attack'. Once again, Dönitz made the point that three to four times the number of U-boats were required in order just to keep pace with the new developments. He also emphasised the likelihood that convoys were using radar to detect U-boats.

9. Wolf Packs Try Again

The need to employ new tactics became paramount as the summer of 1941 progressed. Dönitz could have made his counter moves, involving the introduction of fast moving patrol lines in new operations areas, as early as June had sufficient boats been available. His basic concepts had not changed and the main problem of locating convoys still remained. Once this had been achieved, U-boats could be relied upon to keep in touch for a group attack. To hinder the enemy from locating U-boats, it was decided to keep patrol lines sweeping from east to west over a much larger zone. Previously, U-boats had been restricted to small, well defined areas, and this was thought to have helped Britain detect them.

September to December 1941

The first of these fast moving patrol formations was established early in September 1941 to cover the area between Iceland and the southern tip of Greenland. This soon paid dividends and on the ninth, U85 (OL Eberhard Greger) reported convoy SC42, consisting of about 70 ships and escorts from the 24th Escort Group under Commander Hibband. The subsequent attack might have been more successful had the U-boats been deployed in a tighter formation. As it was, some were too far away and had no hope of reaching the target in time, while fog prevented others from making contact. Nevertheless, 20 ships were reported as sunk and this was looked upon as a definite success. As during earlier actions in 1941, it was noticed that the British had introduced innovations. Escorts were unexpectedly strong in an area so far from land and, for the first time, aircraft were observed to cover the convoy at night.

Though this new attack method was referred to as 'fast moving', U-boats cruised the area at an economical speed of about ten knots, until their target was sighted. Only then were commanders allowed to set any speed they liked. These tactics required more fuel than during earlier operations carried out nearer home and a number of boats left the formation for replenishments in France or Norway. Supply U-boats were not employed until later in the war and the heavy loss of surface ships during June made their employment too risky. The boats with sufficient fuel remaining at sea were directed into the area where convoy SC44 was intercepted by U74 (KK Eitel-Friedrich Kentrat) on 18 September. Several boats were well placed for an attack, but again weather played an important part in

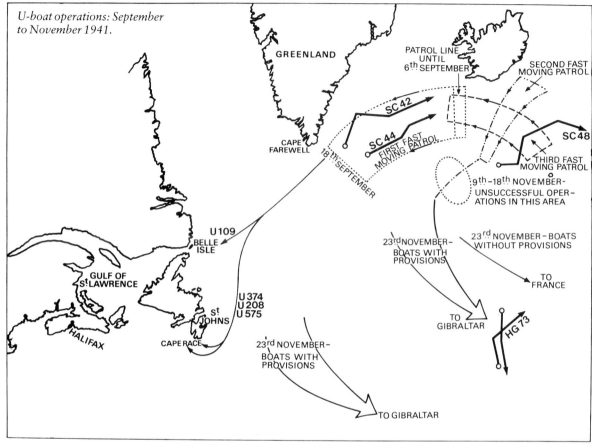

U-boat operations: September to November 1941.

The first fast moving patrol line against convoy SC42		
U38	KK	Heinrich Schuch
U43	KL	Wolfgang Lüth
U81	KL	Friedrich Guggenberger
U82	KL	Siegfried Rollmann
U84	KL	Horst Uphoff
U85	OL	Eberhard Greger
U105	KL	Georg Schewe
U202	KL	Hans-Heinz Linder
U207	OL	Fritz Meyer
U372	KL	Hans-Joachim Neumann (Joined later)
U373	KL	Paul-Karl Loeser
U432	KL	Heinz-Otto Schultze
U433	OL	Hans Ey
U501	KK	Hugo Förster
U552	KK	Erich Topp
U569	KL	Hans-Peter Hinsch
U572	KL	Heinz Hirsacker
U575	KL	Günther Heydemann
U652	OL	Georg-Werner Fraatz

The return leg of the first fast moving patrol line against convoy SC44

U74	KL	Eitel-Friedrich Kentrat
U94	OL	Otto Ites
U373	KL	Paul-Karl Loeser
U552	KL	Erich Topp
U562	KL	Horst Hamm

The following boats followed behind the first fast moving patrol line and went on to reconnoitre Canadian waters:

U109	KL	Heinrich Bleichrodt
U208	OL	Alfred Schlieper
U374	OL	Unno von Fischel
U573	KL	Heinrich Heinsohn

The second fast moving patrol line Established after some of the boats attacked convoy SC48

U73	KL	Helmut Rosenbaum
U77	KL	Heinrich Schonder

U101	KL	Fritz Frauenheim
U432	KL	Heinz-Otto Schultze
U502	KL	Jürgen von Rosenstiel
U553	KK	Karl Thurmann
U558	KL	Günther Krech
U568	KL	Joachim Preuss
U751	KL	Gerhard Bigalk

The third fast moving patrol line against convoy SC52

U38	KK	Heinrich Schuch
U82	KL	Siegfried Rollmann
U84	KL	Horst Uphoff
U85	OL	Eberhard Greger
U93	OL	Horst Elfe
U106	KL	Hermann Rasch
U123	KL	Reinhard Hardegen
U133	KL	Hermann Hesse
U202	KL	Hans-Heinz Linder
U203	KL	Rolf Mützelburg
U569	KL	Hans-Peter Hinsch
U571	KL	Helmut Möhlmann
U577	KL	Herbert Schauenburg

U-boat leathers on the bridge of U109. With his back to the camera is Bootsmaat Walter Gross, next to him Funkmaat Ernst Bischoff and on the left Oberfunkmeister Wolfgang Hirschfeld. Hirschfeld's secret diary is a major contribution to U-boat history. It is especially noteworthy because it was actually written (illegally) in U-boats and in the U-boat Command's radio room, and it is one of the few documents compiled by a person who was not a commissioned officer.

the ensuing action. This time, strong atmospheric interference played havoc with radios and made it impossible to communicate properly and, just before the attack was launched, fog allowed the merchant ships to slip out of the U-boats' fragile grasp.

Although this action consumed more fuel and had the effect of depleting the patrol line further, fresh boats were appearing, making it possible to establish another formation in the second week of October. Plans to intercept convoy OG75 on the second of that month failed because there were too few boats at sea and another two weeks passed before the area between Greenland and Iceland could be scanned with sufficient numbers. U553 (KK Karl Thurmann), on the extreme southern end of the formation, sighted the east-bound convoy SC48 on 15 October, and several boats pursued and attacked it for the next three days. The four northerly boats, identified by the name *Mordbrenner* (Murder Burner) and too far away to reach U553's convoy, were ordered west to investigate traffic conditions around Newfoundland. Another fast moving formation was assembling on the eastern side of the operations area and in order to direct this group, Dönitz urgently needed details of the traffic routes out of the St Lawrence estuary. Boats to the north, off Belle Isle Strait, found nothing and could only curse the rough weather.

To the south, U374 (OL Unno von Fischel) sighted convoy SC52

*Matrosengefreiter Hans
Fehmann of U598 (KL
Gottfried Holtorf) during the
winter. Rain gear, seen here,
was not issued to individuals
but had to be shared.*

off Cape Race and gained some relief from the daily monotony by attacking two ships. The others to the north, such as U109 (KK Ajax Bleichrodt), had no such relief. Morale was at a low ebb, with the men dispirited by their enforced inactivity and the bad weather. Wolfgang Hirschfeld (Radio Operator of U109) summed up the men's feelings in his secret diary: 'We are now the MORDBRENNER Group, with *Schlagetot* (Strike Dead) and *Reisswolf* (Tear Wolf) towards the east, but there is nothing to strike nor to tear at'.

When evaluating the results of the fast moving patrol line, the U-boat Command felt that a tight formation would have a better chance of preventing a convoy from slipping through unseen. Yet, experience had shown the opposite. Only one convoy was detected by a patrol formation, while all the others were discovered by lone boats. Dönitz outlined what he thought to be the reasons for these difficulties that they were having in locating convoys and remarked in passing, 'Coincidence always seems to favour the enemy'. He gave four possible explanations:

1   Betrayal. Everything has been done to reduce this and the people who are informed about U-boat dispositions have been cut down to an absolute minimum. This can hardly be plausible since so few people are informed.
2   By decrypting our radio code. This is constantly tested by the Naval War Staff and is considered to be impossible.
3   Combination of information from radio and sighting reports. We cannot determine this because we do not know how much information is collected by the enemy.
4   Detecting the sources of our broadcasts by radio direction finders or by radar. Information about this is not available at the moment. None of these points really explains the lack of success and we can only continue to keep the patrol formation constantly on the move.

While the tactics involving the fast moving patrol line were being perfected in the north, three disturbing events took place further south. First, KK Johann Mohr, on his maiden voyage as commander of U124, reported the sighting of convoy OG74, heading south with five escorts and, for the first time, an aircraft carrier. This was the hastily converted escort carrier *Audacity* (Commander D W Mackendrick), which made a major contribution to the defeat of U-boats and drove Dönitz to make his famous statement, 'The

The upper foredeck of Types VII differed from Types IX by being considerably narrower. This shows men of U382 secured by safety harnesses working on the 88mm quick-firing gun. Towards the bow of the boat is Oberbootsmannsmaat Sepp Leinenbach, on the left Obersteuermann Sigurd Serger and on the right Maschinengefreiter Kurt Hansen.

chances of U-boats being sunk are greater than the prospects of success'.

Second, a meeting had been arranged for 27 September in Tarafal Bay at the Cape Verde Islands at which U68 (KK Karl-Friedrich Merten) was to collect spare torpedoes from the homeward bound U111 (KL Peter Kleinschmidt). On hearing this, U67 (KL Günther Müller-Stöckheim) asked permission to transfer a sick man to U111 for return to hospital. Standing orders prohibited radio transmissions during the two days before or after a meeting at sea. Therefore, on the day of the rendezvous, the radio room in Kerneval was surprised when U67 suddenly came on the air to report two detonations and a collision with a British submarine. This was followed by another short signal from Kptlt Kleinschmidt, explaining that torpedoes had been handed over and asking whether, in view of enemy presence he could vacate the area without waiting for the sick man. Dönitz replied instantly by ordering the three boats to disperse. As it happened, U67, with the sick man, had to return as well. The collision with HM Submarine *Clyde* (David Ingram) put three of the four bow torpedo tubes on U67 out of action and though the damage was not serious, it was too difficult to repair at sea. The most disturbing question was how the Royal Navy knew about the meeting. Again, Dönitz asked the Naval War Staff to tighten radio procedure and further suggested that a traitor might be responsible for this unwelcome incident.

U-Oesten coming alongside Anneliese Essberger. During the war, U-boat numbers were confidential and boats were usually referred to by the name of the commanding officer. This is U106 (KL Jürgen Oesten) which had gone out to escort the blockade breaker for the last leg of its dangerous voyage.

The third disturbing event came on 4 October when U129 (KL Nicolai Clausen) reported having picked up 119 men from the U-boat supply ship *Kota Pinang*, which had been sunk the previous day by the Royal Navy cruiser *Kenya*. Two days later, the survivors were handed over to a Spanish tug, and operations in the far southern Atlantic had to be cancelled due to the lack of a provisions source.

Meanwhile, October continued with poor results and on the last day of the month U81 (KL Friedrich Guggenberger) reported that he was unable to dive as a result of an aircraft attack. Dönitz immediately asked the Naval High Command for air and surface support to help the crippled boat to France, but assistance was not possible. The distance to the western side of the Bay of Biscay was beyond the range of fighter aircraft and nothing larger could be made available. Furthermore ships were tied up in port and this left Dönitz with no choice but to direct two operational U-boats, U201 (OL Günther Rosenberg) and U98 (KK Wilhelm Schulze), to the area. U81's crew managed to patch up the damage and crawl slowly home but the incident left the U-boat Command with a bitter feeling. It was bad for morale to know that injured men had to run the risk of being sunk on their own door step. Dönitz emphasised that as the Biscay area was bound to attract an ever increasing enemy presence, something had to be done to provide basic escorts for damaged boats. This was only one example of several similar incidents which occurred throughout the summer of 1941 which the U-boat Command perceived as serious problems.

A week later, Dönitz was in Berlin for discussions with the Supreme Commander-in-Chief of the Navy to clear the air on a number of points. He emphasised that the days of lone merchant-men being found were over and that convoys were becoming more difficult to find and to attack. More boats were urgently required and the scattering of the available submarines over a wide area needed to be avoided. The shortage of repair workers was also giving great cause for concern. Other problems included the dire shortage of vessels, used to catch torpedoes, at the training establishments. Since the beginning of the war their numbers had been reduced by a third. The meeting closed with Raeder promising to bring these matters to the attention of the Führer.

There were still considerable differences of opinion between Dönitz and the Supreme Naval Command. For example, on 1 November he was asked to divert six boats from the North Atlantic to serve as escorts for surface ships. Dönitz remarked that such duties, involving long hours of fast cruising, consumed great quantities of fuel and seriously curtailed the action radius of the boats. A day later, the Naval War Staff ordered eight boats into Polar regions. Four of them were to carry out exploratory activities. Dönitz asked, 'Is it really worth it? They sink nothing up there and achieve little!' Protests were to no avail and ten days later the Naval War Staff asked for another four boats to be posted in the Atlantic as weather stations, although four were already there.

A burning tanker of convoy PQ18 seen from U405.

On 23 November 1941 came one of the biggest blows to Dönitz's plans when he was ordered to send every boat east, either into the Mediterranean or to be positioned west of Gibraltar. By 27 November, not a single boat remained in the North Atlantic and Dönitz's efforts in the important shipping lanes came to a complete standstill. A few weeks earlier, Dönitz had half jokingly predicted this, saying, 'The war in the Atlantic is rapidly slowing down. It will probably soon grind to a complete halt'. Now, exactly that had happened and Britain was given a most welcome break.

To lower morale in U-boat headquarters yet further, there came the news of the sinking of the auxiliary cruiser *Atlantis* (KS Bernhard Rogge) in the South Atlantic. It had just been ordered to cease activities as a surface raider and concentrate on the role of supply ship for submarines. The Royal Navy, being able to understand the U-boat code, dispatched the cruiser *Devonshire* (Cpt Oliver) to the rendezvous to sink Germany's first disguised raider on its 622nd day at sea. The distress signal, sent by *Atlantis* in regulation British code, was picked up by the B-Dienst and the U-boat supply ship *Python* (Kpt Lueders) was diverted to pick up survivors. The survivors had been initially picked up by U126 (KL Ernst Bauer),

KL Rolf-Heinrich Hopman (wearing a white hat) of U405 watching smoke from a burning ship in convoy PQ18

which was being supplied when *Devonshire* appeared. *Python's* arrival in far southern waters was a welcome surprise for the U-boat Command and Dönitz remarked that four boats would soon be ready to operate off Cape Town. His enthusiasm was shortlived, however, and on 1 December plans were cancelled. *Python* had been sunk as well.

To crown these disappointments, Admiral Hans Georg von Friedeburg (Commander-in-Chief of the Organisation Department of the U-boat Arm) announced at Christmas that the shortage of workers had resulted in finishing off work taking from six to nine weeks, instead of the two to four weeks in which it had been achieved before. Von Friedeburg suggested that matters could be improved if the calling up of skilled workers for national service was stopped. The unskilled men and women who were brought in as replacements took much longer in completing the work and often produced inferior results. For the U-boat Command, the year ended on a low note.

10. Five Boats versus the United States

December 1941 to April 1942

Shortly after the Japanese attack on Pearl Harbor on 7 December 1941 and the German declaration of war against the United States, the U-boat Command asked permission to send 12 long-range Type IX to American waters. The Naval War Staff replied by saying that the numbers off Gibraltar and in the Mediterranean could not be reduced and gave permission for only six boats to be made ready. In the event only five actually sailed.

Although planning an engagement against the United States occupied all the staff and involved considerable time, Dönitz wanted simultaneously to resume the convoy war in the North Atlantic, which had been abandoned in November; but the number of available U-boats meant that the battle would be waged with fewer U-boats than had been available at the beginning of the war. The operational fleet consisted of 91 boats. Thirty-seven of these were at sea, but only 18 were in a position to strike. Nineteen were either on their way out or homeward-bound. Of the other 54 boats, the majority were held up in ports awaiting repairs. There appeared to be no likelihood of any immediate reduction in the number of boats in port and to make matters even worse, five days after these figures had been compiled, Admiral Hans-Georg von Friedeburg (Commander-in-Chief of the U-boats' Organisation Department) reported that he could no longer forecast the number of new boats coming to the front. Skilled workers and other shipyard employees were still being called up for service with the armed forces and it was impossible to predict future completion dates.

On 11 January 1942, a short time before the start of the famous Operation Paukenschlag (A roll on the kettle drums), Dönitz recorded his views on the forthcoming sortie into United States waters. He expected to encounter mainly lone ships with strong defences, especially in the air, but he argued that as anti-U-boat forces had hardly had time to prepare themselves, there was a good chance that fruitful gains might be made. The element of surprise was on the German side. It was considered of paramount import-ance for all boats to attack simultaneously otherwise it was thought that the second U-boat would run into a trap triggered by the first. It has often been thought that Dönitz wanted to strike a hard and impressive blow against the eastern seaboard of the United States

U889 (KL Friedrich Braeucker), a long-distance boat of Type IXC, undergoing trials shortly after the war under the White Ensign. The boat surrendered at Shelbourne in Canada and was handed over to the United States before being scrapped.

and the code name Operation Paukenschlag was perhaps partly responsible for perpetrating this myth. In fact, exactly the opposite was true. Dönitz was under no illusion as to the likely success of the operation. Indeed, he genuinely feared the virtual annihilation of all boats which dared approach too close. So Operation Paukenschlag was planned as a quick series of simultaneous attacks which would deny the enemy any chance of retaliation.

Today it is well known how the United States was not only unprepared for the U-boat onslaught, but was also loathe to take countermeasures for fear of upsetting the coastal holiday trade. Lights were kept on, ships continued to sail as in peacetime and even radio was used openly for U-boats to listen in. On 8 February, KL Reinhard Hardegen (U123) reported back to U-boat headquarters saying the situation was more akin to peacetime, with ships continuously coming into the sights. Dönitz thanked him for his efforts but warned, 'This placid situation will not last. The next wave must be prepared for strong defences'.

Initial news of successes was transmitted back by radio and Dönitz immediately made plans to utilise what he thought would be a short temporary advantage. New boats on their way to the North Western Approaches of Great Britain were instructed to abandon their plans and make for France at fastest possible speed to be fitted out for crossing the Atlantic. Once again, a good move by the U-boat Command was partially frustrated by higher authorities. This time Hitler intervened. He envisaged a possible invasion of Norway and he ordered the navy to send U-boats into Norwegian waters as a front line of defence against any enemy attack.

Dönitz also wanted to keep other operational areas under constant review. U132 (KL Ernst Vogelsang) was ordered to make for Reykjavik to survey merchant traffic, while U505 (KL Axel-Olaf Loewe) and U68 (KK Karl-Friedrich Merten) were made ready to go south into the shipping lanes off Freetown. It was thought that the African waters might yield good pickings after the dissolution of the Pan American Neutrality Zone and enemy traffic might be tempted to move further east into the shorter prewar trade routes between South America and Europe. The U-boat Command was also considering moving south of Florida to the Caribbean to avoid anticipated retaliation in northern United States waters, and merchant marine officers were consulted as to the best places to strike. However, the new boats earmarked for the Caribbean were ordered to go to Norway instead.

On 31 January 1941, U96 (KK Heinrich Lehmann-Willenbrock) sailed from Germay to Canadian waters, ending up in the same area as KL Günther Heydemann (U575), who had sailed a fortnight earlier from France. In an attempt to avoid the cold northern weather, both boats headed further south and at the end of February they had reached the New York area. There they reported to be operating against extremely limited defences and suffered only minimal harassment from aircraft. Most important, both boats still had an adequate supply of fuel. Although it was possible to calculate theoretical ranges, it was always difficult to be accurate when dealing with such long distances; currents, weather patterns, the amount of fuel used to avoid attackers and the boat's own quirks could not be calculated. Officers at U-boat headquarters were quite surprised to learn that the small VIIC boats had got that far with so little fuel, especially as U123 (a Type IXB under KL

A Type VIIC boat at speed. The loop on the top of the conning tower is a radio direction finder aerial. Forward of the 88mm quick-firing gun is the receiver of the underwater sound detection gear. This could hear propeller noises when the ships were beyond the lookout's horizon, but it only worked when the submarine was dived.

Erich Topp, who commanded U57 and the Red Devil Boat (U552). Topp was one of the most decorated U-boat commanders, having been awarded the Knights Cross of the Iron Cross with Oakleaves and Swords. Later, he became a Flotilla Chief, commander of U2513 (an electro-boat of Type XXI) and an Admiral in the Federal German Navy.

Reinhard Hardegen) had not performed as well as had been anticipated. U96 and U575 certainly proved that it would be possible for Type VII boats to operate there and plans went ahead to station a tanker to the east of New York. The experiences during February also convinced Dönitz that the New York area was suitable for training new U-boat crews. The weak defences made it ideal for inexperienced crews to practise for the harder battles which were bound to follow.

A short time later Dönitz summarised his general impressions by saying that the defences were poor and Americans untrained and badly organised in all the areas except off the Canadian coast between Halifax and Cape Race. Air defences were present but were poor compared with the British. It was thought that further risks could be reduced by stationing a supply vessel east of New York thereby reducing the number of perilous Atlantic crossings. There appeared to be no quick responses to U-boats going close inshore and the flow of merchant traffic continued as if that was no threat. Only occasionally were sailings stopped, and then it appeared more a result of a shock reaction than a carefully planned manoeuvre. There were many lone sailings and a high proportion of these were tankers.

After exactly four months of the war against the United States, KL Reinhard Hardegen (U123) – the man who started it by sinking the British freighter *Cyclops* – reported to Dönitz again, saying Cape Hatteras resembled a carnival with the sort of bright illuminations that might be encountered in peacetime, but Hardegen and Dönitz agreed that defences had become stronger, with a noticeable increase in the number of patrol boats, especially off Cape Hatteras. The U-boats' success rates, however, were still as high as four months earlier and as yet no U-boat had been sunk or even seriously damaged on that side of the Atlantic. Dönitz thought the Americans were careless, inexperienced, and not determined enough when chasing U-boats. They did not appear to be fighting back.

It took the United States a considerable time to face up to the carnage of the merchant marine. For a long time, men continued to sail without any significant precautions being taken to prevent their annihilation. Immediately after the war, the heavy losses off Cape Hatteras were explained as being the result of a large concentration of U-boats. Professor Samuel Eliot Morison in *The Atlantic Battle Won* described the attack as 'a merry massacre' and in 1946, though he could not determine how many U-boats were responsible, suggested that in January there was a daily average of 19. In fact, there were only five and one of those (U109 KL Ajax Bleichrodt) had already used up some torpedoes in Canadian waters. In addition, all the boats were plagued by a number of torpedo failures.

Successes throughout the first quarter of 1942 were again marred by several reports of torpedo failures. U553 (KK Karl Thurmann) had seven failures against one ship; U552 (KK Erich Topp) five failures; U654 (OL Ludwig Forster) seven failures in nine shots and many other boats reported two or three failures. The torpedo mechanic onboard U654 discovered a novel fault when he found that the torpedo batteries inside the tubes could be accidentally connected to the boat's heating system, causing a short circuit which quickly drained them. This fault hardly explained the numerous failures, however, and Dönitz remarked, 'The number of failures is unusually high and some of them must be put down to mechanical breakdown'.

Heinz Frisch, the cook. For many men of U355 he was the most important member of the crew. Behind him is the after edge of the conning tower with navigation light.

The move into United States waters brought further ructions between the U-boat Command and the Naval War Staff. This was triggered by Dönitz saying, 'It does not seem right to employ so many boats on side shows where they are not sinking anything. If these boats were stationed off America, they would achieve much higher success rates'. The Naval War Staff took exception to the statement, expressing their strong objections over two pages of A4.

Even when trying to be helpful, the Naval War Staff were capable of upsetting the U-boat Command. In March, it was suggested that U-boats be moved to Norway for final training. This would carry with it the advantage of enabling fully trained and operational boats to be released from duty there and sent out into the Atlantic. Dönitz objected on the grounds that the fiords were too limited for training and he stuck to his belief that the Baltic was a better training ground for U-boat crews. The value of training in such a protected sea before going out into the vastness of the Atlantic is open to question. The Royal Navy appeared to have had a slightly different attitude. When crews for the X-Craft were trained for the attack on the battleship *Tirpitz* in northern Norway, two battleships were moved into Scottish sea lochs to act as training targets Bearing in mind that these ships were in short supply and that an old broken hulk or canvas stretched over a raft could have been used, it shows that the Royal Navy put great emphasis upon reality in training.

March 1942 ended with the U-boat Command moving back to Paris. This came about after a direct order from Hitler to move all headquarters to safe locations away from front lines. Dönitz was initially wary of such a move believing that it would cut the close bond with the men at sea and he played for time by asking for clarification of what was considered safe. Two days later, at 0250 hours on 28 March, he was woken by the telephone with the news of an allied landing in St Nazaire. This British commando raid resulted in Dönitz ordering all boats east of 29° West to make for St Nazaire without delay and it illustrated the vulnerability of the U-boat headquarters. The move to Paris was made on 30 March 1942. For the time being, the radio transmitters remained in Kerneval and it took only ten minutes for messages to be relayed to Paris.

*   *   *

On the eastern side of the Atlantic, several interesting developments took place. On 31 January, U105 (KL Heinrich Schuch), a long-range boat of Type IXB, ran into convoy SL93 while en route to American waters. Taking the opportunity to attack, Schuch found himself quickly driven off by escorts. A subsequent duel ended with the sloop *Culver* being sunk and U105 being forced to turn back for repairs. No one in U105 knew that *Culver* was the first ship to be equipped with an automatic high frequency direction finder (HF/DF).

Another significant convoy attack occurred on 21 February, after a chance encounter between U155 (KK Adolf Piening) and 36 ships of the outward-bound convoy ON67. An HF/DF fitted in the British 1571 GRT rescue ship *Toward* made it possible to direct escorts towards the approaching U-boat. The escorts themselves were not equipped with radar and, although close to the U-boat, were unable to see it approaching on the surface. Piening managed to shoot four torpedoes during the last hours of darkness of the twenty-second though without success. Following this, the U-boat Command ordered him to maintain contact, to guide in a group of five outward-bound boats, all with inexperienced commanders and men, who happened to be passing through the area bound for Canada. KL Günther Krech (U558) made three separate attacks and sank four ships. U158 (KL Erich Rostin) attacked two stragglers, while U587 (KL Ulrich Borcherdt) and U558 (KL Günther Krech) attacked a number of ships but only managed to sink one between them. The other member of the group, OL Otto Ites (U94, at one time 2WO in the famous U48), sank the 7005 GRT *Empire*

Hail some distance behind the convoy. All the attacking boats managed to achieve some success, which demonstrated that the young commanders could achieve results despite their lack of experience. (Krech was longest in command, having commissioned U558 in February 1941 and the others had only taken command in September 1941.)

In February 1942, U-boats scored two own goals. The first was announced on Sunday the first, by a terse broadcast from Dönitz: 'To all U-boats. Who sank a ship in square CB4965?' This was followed by, 'To all U-boats. The German blockade breaker *Spreewald* is sending an SOS from north of the Azores'. A few hours later came an unusually long broadcast from U333 (KL Ali Cremer) with a detailed description of an attack and the target. The U-boat Command replied almost instantly, 'Cremer, you have sunk the German steamer *Spreewald*'. Wolfgang Hirschfeld (onboard U109) finished his secret diary for that day with, 'Cremer will hear more when he gets home. It is a tragedy'. *Spreewald* (Kapitän Bull) had left Dairen in China on 21 October 1941, was replenished from the supply ship *Kulmerland* and was just a short distance from a rendezvous with her U-boat escort (U575, KL Günther Heydemann) when she ran into the sights of U333. Günter Hessler (U-boat Command Staff Officer and Dönitz's son-in-law) demonstrated that *Spreewald* had created a misunderstanding by failing to give its position and consequently the correct details had not been relayed to U333. At his court martial, Cremer was found not guilty and he went on to become one of the most famous U-boat Commanders of the war. He also has the unique distinction of being the only commander to have collided with four ships on four separate occasions and each time to have brought his wrecked boat home.

The second own goal was less disastrous since both parties managed to reach home without loss of life. The incident occurred on the American side of the Atlantic during a spell of poor visibility when U564 (KL Teddy Suhren) ran into U107 (KL Harald Gelhaus), damaging the fuel tank which contained most of her oil. U564 had to refuel Gelhaus before both of them could return for repairs. U107 was unable to continue her mission because the external doors to all four bow torpedo tubes were jammed shut. There was considerable relief at U-boat Command at the safe return of the two vessels and no further action was taken against the commanders.

U586 (KL Dietrich von der Esch) negotiating the Kiel Canal. Near the bow of the boat, sticking up above the deck, is a detachable windlass which could be rotated electrically from below or manually from on deck.

11. Defeat in Victory

The British successes of 1941, largely a result of the ability to decipher U-boat radio codes, led the German High Command to believe, falsely, that the Allies' numbers had increased sufficiently for even remote areas to be patrolled. Although he subscribed to this view, Dönitz pointed to the strange fact that the apparent coincidence of ships running into each other always seemed to favour the enemy and, suggesting that such incidents resulted from Britain understanding his secret code, asked for a thorough check on all radio procedures. VA Erhard Maertens (head of the Communications Department at the Supreme Naval Command) put the encounters down to chance and poor lookouts and maintained that there was no real evidence to suggest that the cypher system had been compromised. Earlier in the war Dönitz had accepted such views, but his earlier experiences with the torpedo problem had made him sceptical of the hierarchy and this led him to question the experts and to demand a new radio code for the Atlantic. Consequently, on 1 February 1942, a revised system, named TRITON, replaced HYDRA.

The Germans could not have chosen a worse time for the switch. Their U-boats had been out of the Atlantic shipping lanes since the latter days of November 1941 and the year 1942 saw the move into American waters, which led to a period of notable success, known as The Second Golden Time. So when the new code was introduced, the turbulent transformation in the general pattern of the war prevented anyone in Germany noticing an intelligence blackout in London which began in February. Had the change been made a few months either side of February 1942, it could have been done during convoy operations and Germany might have noticed Britain's sudden inability to locate U-boats. By the time operations returned to the air gap (ie the area free from land-based aircraft) of the mid-Atlantic in summer 1942, another change in the pattern of war led the German High Command to think their procedures were secure. Then, in the autumn of 1942 when Britain started to re-gain an insight into the U-boat code, Germany thought their radio secrets were safe and started to explore several red herrings in the hope of finding information about how the enemy detected U-boats. At the same time, the German High Command was more than ever convinced of the increased numbers of escorts.

U552, the Red Devil Boat seen through its own periscope. The object at the bow looks like a scarecrow or it could be an effigy of the red devil.

In June, following the first successes in the air gap of the mid-Atlantic, Dönitz stated, 'There has been no change in the pattern of the war at sea. Only the enemy's intensification of action in the Bay of Biscay has become an intimidating new threat'. Günter Hessler and Alfred Hoschatt went further when they wrote, 'The summer of 1942 saw a change in emphasis from finding convoys to attacking them'. Despite the promising resumption of anti-convoy activity in summer 1942, during the Special Intelligence blackout in London, far-reaching changes were afoot and only three months later on 28 September, Dönitz presented a disturbing report to the Supreme Naval Command stating, 'There is ample evidence to suggest the enemy has gained the upper hand'.

This drastic change of view within such a short period was due to a combination of factors which centred around the new radio code. The total intelligence blackout in London placed the Royal Navy in almost the same predicament that it had faced during the 'Happy Period' of autumn 1940, but by 1942 Britain had developed various ways of combating the threat. The most noteworthy of the new developments was the introduction of specially adapted tankers to refuel escorts at sea. In addition, provisions were made to allow merchant ships to make drastic changes in course once shadowing U-boats were located. As the British came to understand the way in which wolf packs attacked, they were able to utilise escorts to better effect and to have inner and outer defensive rings which made it much more difficult for shadowing U-boats to keep contact. Anti-submarine weapons had also been improved and an increase in the number of escorts deployed on convoy duties allowed the Royal Navy to pursue U-boats much more rigorously, often to extinction.

The combination of these factors, together with a small supply of Special Intelligence, helped at least four convoys (OS33, SC97, SC99 and SL118), having been caught by patrol lines, to escape before the pack could be brought to attack. Special Intelligence continued to trickle into the secret submarine tracking room in London because the new German radio code introduced in February 1942 only applied to the Atlantic. Coastal traffic, especially escorts in and out of harbours continued to use the old HYDRA system, so Britain could, for example, work out when U-boats were setting out from their bases. Being able to determine the latitude of the signal and knowing the speed of the boats made it possible to estimate where they were going and when they would arrive.

The intensification of British activities in the Bay of Biscay, mentioned earlier, was clearly evidenced by the loss of three experienced boats. U502 (KL Jürgen von Rosenstiel) was lost to Bay Air Patrols on 5 July, U751 (KL Gerhard Bigalk) on 17 July and U578 (KK Ernst-August Rehwinkel) on 9 August. In addition to these, the U-boat Command was aware of more than half a dozen less experienced boats having been lost to aircraft. Two of them, U166 (Ol Hans Günter Kuhlmann) and U261 (KL Hans Lange) had been in service for less than five months, including their training. U705 (KL Karl-Horst Horn) had seen eight months service and the other boats about eleven months. In addition to these losses, many more boats were damaged. For example, in June, U753 (KK Manhardt von Mannstein) only just managed to get back after an aircraft attack. Shortly before this, U105 (KK Heinrich Schuch) had less luck, being forced to put into El Ferrol in Spain. To add to their troubles U-boat Command was forced to divert up to half a dozen U-boats from their planned operations to assist colleagues in danger. The Bay of Biscay had become what the U-boat Command called, 'The great playground for the Royal Air Force, where heavy

The upper after deck of U181 when on its way to Penang under KK Kirt Freiwald. Much of the deck planking was washed away by a storm and revealed a variety of pressure-resistant storage containers above the pressure hull.

bombers could romp about at will without interference'. Dönitz said, 'It is sad and depressing for U-boat crews to know that virtually nothing can be offered to help disabled boats back to port and to protect them from further attack. The situation is now so bad that there are more boats in port awaiting repairs than there are at the front'. This caustic complaint yielded some results. The Luftwaffe Commander for the Atlantic gained another 24 aircraft. As immediate countermeasure, boats were ordered to cross the Bay of Biscay submerged, and only to surface in order to recharge their batteries. Despite the losses, Dönitz felt that U-boats could win the war against aircraft and in August he stated, 'In the long run, aeroplanes cannot harm submarines'.

The U-boat Command's disturbing report of 28 September to the Supreme Naval Command resulted in an immediate meeting between Hitler, Raeder and Dönitz in Berlin, which was in itself an unusual event. It was common for Grand Admiral Erich Raeder (Supreme Commander-in-Chief of the Navy) to present regular situation reports and he was often accompanied by KS Jesko von Puttkammer (Hitler's Naval Adjutant) and VA Theodor Krancke (Permanent Naval Representative at the Führer's headquarters), but few naval commanders were introduced to Hitler's headquarters. It would seem that Dönitz was one of the first commanders to meet Hitler with the sole objective of presenting his case and

*The foredeck of U73 (KL
Helmut Rosenbaum) rolling
through lively seas.*

arguing a number of specific points. Previously, he had only met
Hitler at official functions and once, when he had lectured in the
Führer's presence, a large audience had prevented him from ex-
pressing the views which he would have made in private.

Hitler opened the September meeting by acknowledging the
U-boats' successes and predicting good results for the future and he
felt certain that the enemy could not replace all the lost tonnage
though it was clear that many merchant seamen were being rescued
and thus able to man new ships. Hitler also made it clear that he
appreciated the need to keep up to date with technical developments and to promote new weapons to the front quickly. After that
Dönitz presented a picture of recent developments and concluded
with the following suggestions and requests. First, the high-speed
Walter boat, with its closed circuit engine, should be given high
priority as it was the only vehicle capable of penetrating convoy
defences. Second, existing submarines should be modified for deeper diving in order to reduce the effectiveness of depth charges and
Asdic. Third, an anti-destroyer weapon, in the form of an acoustic
torpedo, was urgently needed. At this stage Raeder interrupted to
say that the new magnetic detonator, already being supplied, was
intended to explode under the target to break its back and that it
was likely to cause considerably more damage than the percussion
types which had been in use up until then. (Magnetic detonators

had been used at the beginning of the war, but were abandoned after numerous failures during the Norwegian Campaign of 1940.) Fourth, Dönitz asked that remote controlled, rocket propelled anti-aircraft defences be provided for surfaced submarines. Hitler cut in to explain that the army's and air force's developments in these fields must be viewed in an optimistic light, and that Dönitz should not count on any of their projects being completed in the near future. Fifth, with the increasing threat of attack from the air, Dönitz asked for more anti-aircraft armament in the form of 15mm machine guns. Hitler, however, thought these guns not powerful enough to tackle modern fast flying and armoured planes and objected to the suggestion of using 37mm and 50mm automatic guns as the Luftwaffe had found them unsatisfactory. The problems associated with saltwater corrosion were discussed and Hitler, who saw the need for guns to be ready for instant action after surfacing, assured Dönitz that less corrodible metals would be made available for weapon construction. The last point which Dönitz raised was the U-boats' poor radius of vision and he asked for more aircraft to be deployed in the Atlantic. VA Werner Lange (Head of the U-boat Division at the Supreme Naval Command) outlined recent research into this problem and said that there were two possible solutions that were almost ready for operational trials. The first consisted of a ten-metre high lookout mast attached to the conning tower and the second an autogyro (the Focke-Achgelis, code named Bachstelze) towed by the U-boat.

Following a lengthy discussion regarding the mounting of a hangar on U-boats to carry a reconnaissance plane, Hitler went on to suggest a special torpedo to feign sinking, noting that large patches of oil were usually reported as evidence of a U-boat having been sunk. He suggested a torpedo, containing old oil and a few explosives, be ejected to put pursuers off the scent of the real boat. Dönitz objected on the grounds that valuable torpedo space would be lost and that escorts would almost certainly continue to search with their Asdic.

Asdic and radar were hardly discussed at this meeting because both topics had already come to a head earlier in the summer of 1942 and countermeasures were under way. Earlier in the war, attempts had been made to absorb audible Asdic impulses by coating submarines with a layer of absorbent rubber. The first trials with this so-called Alberich Skin were carried out on U11 (KL Georg Peters) and later with the much larger U67 (KL Ajax Bleichrodt and later KL Günther Müller-Stöckheim). More than 50

U664 (OL Adolf Graef) on passage through the Kiel Canal. Commanders who knew this sea route went through on their own, otherwise canal pilots were supplied to negotiate this narrow waterway. Sticking up above the conning tower are the attack periscope on the right and the loop of the radio direction finder, which could determine the direction from which radio signals were coming. It was used for homing in on U-boats shadowing convoys.

percent of the matting was washed off during the first cruise and the remainder simply flapped against the sides. When intact, the skin produced good results, but the difficulties of applying it in dust-free and dry conditions and its easy removal by seawater led the Germans to abandon the project. Instead they concentrated on decoys. Asdic foxers had been requested as early as mid 1941 and were made as 15cm-diameter tins which could be ejected through a purpose-built tube in the side of the rear torpedo compartment. The mass of bubbles, produced on contact with seawater, was intended to confuse Asdic operators.

During the autumn of 1942, radar and radar detection equipment were still in an embryonic state. An investigation during the summer of that year concluded that escorts were not using radar.

Yet only five months later, the Germans considered radar detectors to be essential for operations in the Atlantic. This sudden change of attitude had come about due to the much improved use of radar by the crews of allied surface ships. At first, escorts would go off at high speed once their equipment produced a response. The efficiency of the radar decreased the closer it came to the target because the time between transmission of the signal and picking up its echo decreased until eventually the two merged. Consequently, radar contact was lost at about the time the escort appeared on the U-boat's horizon and from then on it had to rely on lookouts to detect the target. At this point the low submarine had the advantage of being better able to keep an eye on the bulkier ship. Many commanders reported escorts coming towards them at fast speeds and, not knowing the position of the U-boat, continuing straight past and on into the darkness. On identifying this problem, the Royal Navy changed its tactics and the ship with radar stayed on its original course while another escort was sent off to investigate the contact. Very High Frequency (VHF) radios, whose transmissions could only be picked up in line of sight, were introduced for quick communications between ships.

Although the subject of radar had been on some German minds since before the war, the U-boat Command did not recognise the significance of radio detection until surprise attacks from aircraft in the Bay of Biscay became more frequent. From the summer of 1942, sudden appearances of the Royal Air Force started to become a worrying factor and tests carried out in September by U128 (KL Hermann Steinert) confirmed that the opposition was using radar to detect U-boats. As a countermeasure, German experts suggested the installation of a receiver to pick up these radar signals and thus warn U-boats of aircraft around them. Known as Metox, after the firm which made the first sets, the early aerials consisted of simple wooden crosses with wires strung around the outside. As more radar detectors came to the front, the so-called Biscay Crosses were replaced by better aerials on the conning towers. The design of the equipment was kept simple to help speed up production and it produced excellent results. U107 (KL Harald Gelhaus), one of the first boats to sail with a Metox radar detector and Biscay Cross, reported several signals, but not a single attack. Initially, the shortage of equipment meant that outward-bound boats passed their sets as well as the trained operator to homeward-bound colleagues. The few radar detectors which later found their way into the North Atlantic were put to good use for locating aircraft around convoys. At the same time they produced the disturbing evidence that allied surface vessels were also using radar. Only a few months earlier an enquiry had led the U-boat Command to believe the exact opposite.

12. More Worries, Problems and Frustrations

January to September 1942

Now, more than 40 years after the war and with access to documents from both sides, it is relatively easy to analyse events and to isolate significant incidents and developments. However, at the time things were not so clear and the U-boat command certainly pursued a number of red herrings which led to some questionable decisions being made. One of the first distractions of 1942, the introduction by the British of Q-ships, came to a head in April. Q-ships, disguised merchant raiders with hidden anti-submarine weapons, had been deployed during World War I and early in 1942 there were strong indications to suggest such vessels were back at sea. On 6 February, U82 (KL Siegfried Rollmann) vanished from the Azores area. Other losses included U587 (KL Ulrich Borcherdt) on 27 March and U252 (KL Kai Lerchen) on 14 April. In each case the U-boats had reported a small convoy on an unusual heading, which had not been identified by the B-Dienst. Thinking that a hunter killer group was underway, U-boats were ordered on 19 April to avoid convoys between 43° and 50°North and between 10° and 15°West. The convoys responsible for this error of identification appear to have been OS18, WS17 and OG82. They consisted, in fact, of normal merchant ships following the usual admiralty instructions and the sinister element probably crept in simply because of inaccurate course headings relayed by the U-boats. Furthermore, stories of special anti-submarine auxiliary cruisers were prompted by examples of fierce resistance from merchantmen who were not prepared to give in to a U-boat without a fight. For example, there was a reversal of roles on 7 July when U109 (KL Ajax Bleichrodt) was chased by the 8336 GRT British freighter *City of Auckland*, after the first torpedo had failed to sink her. Eventually, the ship ran off at speed while making smoke and the men in U109 were not certain whether this had been triggered off by their own deck gun or generated for the purposes of cover. The remarkable point was that a ship of 1914 vintage should be equipped with expensive smoke generating apparatus. On 26 March, KL Reinhard Hardegen (U123) had been faced with a similar situation, when he failed to sink the US freighter *Carolyn*, as a result of considerable opposition from her.

After April 1942, when retaliation made the waters off Cape Hatteras untenable, Dönitz moved the smaller boats back into the air gap in the mid-Atlantic and the larger ones south to the coasts of Florida and into the Caribbean. To prevent American submarine chasers following, it was also necessary to maintain a presence in the north and mine-layers were considered to be best for this role. The first of the large (Type XB) mine-layers, U116 (KK Werner von Schmidt), which had been commissioned a year earlier in July 1941, stirred up a mass of trouble. Up until this time, U-boats laid specially small (750-800 kg) mines through their torpedo tubes. Three TMB mines (Torpedo Mine Type B) or two TMA mines were the same length as a standard torpedo, thus three TMB or two TMA could be fitted into one tube. It was thought to be too dangerous to re-load during the laying of a barrage and it was often considered best to keep at least one torpedo loaded for self defence, so the number of mines available for laying at any one time was limited by these tactical considerations rather than by the boats' capacities. Minelayers of Type XB and VIID had a different arrangement. They carried larger SMA (Shaft Mine Type A) mines in vertical shafts. First trials showed up a glaring fault which caused some of the mines to detonate within seconds of leaving their tubes and this had not been rectified by the time Dönitz wanted to start a mining offensive in the United States. Once again he had to initiate a mission on a much smaller scale than he would have liked. The first wave of mine-layers, consisting of U87 (KL Joachim Berger), U373 (KL Paul-Karl Loeser) and U701 (KL Horst Degen), left France on 19 May to mine New York, Delaware Bay and Chesapeake Bay respectively. (U87 was a Type VIIB and the other two VIICs.) The last mentioned target area was changed to Cape Henry as a number of freighters destined for neutral ports and carrying cargo for Germany were passing through Chesapeake Bay. After these three missions, which Dönitz considered to have been successful, more mining ventures were organised and a few unsuccessful operations continued throughout 1942. It is not clear, however, how he came to regard these three missions as successful: U701 has only been credited with sinking five ships, U373 with one tug and U87 with nothing.

While these mining operations were under way, three sorties to land agents were carried out. This task was particularly disliked by Dönitz because he considered these particular men to be adventurers rather than serious agents and there was always a risk that they might divulge U-boat secrets to bargain for better conditions once they were captured. Such operations were ordered by the Supreme

Dietrich von der Esch (U586) in February 1942. The badge on the side of his hat, depicting an iron hand, originated during a depth charge attack, when someone remarked that it sounded like a giant banging on the hull with a steel fist

OL Herbert Brammer commissioning U1060, a Type VIIF. In the background is a 20mm anti-aircraft gun and the flag served as ensign to the Kriegsmarine.

Command of the Armed Forces (OKW) and the navy was obliged to provide the transport. There was little the U-boat Command could do to object. U252 (KL Kai Lerchen) landed the first of the groups in Iceland on 8 April. This was followed on 13 June by a landing from U202 (KL Hans-Heinz Linder) at Long Island near New York and five days later U584 (KL Joachim Deecke) landed men near Jacksonville. The agents went ashore in rubber dinghies and all were captured shortly after their arrival, only adding fuel to the U-boat men's dislike of such clandestine operations. The U-boats had been specially prepared for their uninvited guests in order to prevent them gaining too much insight into submarine routines or any information concerning other boats.

*   *   *

Bearing in mind that a considerable effort was required to obtain permission to start the American offensive with half a dozen boats, Dönitz must have been surprised when on 6 June, the Supreme Naval Command ordered him to prepare 15 boats for a simultaneous attack against Brazil. He responded by asking where he was to find such a large concentration of submarines. Then he told his superiors, 'Such an undertaking can only be performed if a tanker is stationed in southern waters and none is available for the immediate future'. Protest was to no avail; despite all the difficulties the

U354 (probably under Karl-Heinz Herbschleb, although Hans-Jürgen Sthamer also commanded the boat), an Atlantic boat of Type VIIC, running into Norway. This flash picture emphasises the shortage of daylight in northern latitudes during winter months, when boats never saw the sun. The badge of the 11th U-Flotilla, showing a polar bear and U-boat, can be seen on the side of the tower.

attack was to begin on 20 June. The officers at U-boat headquarters had hardly overcome their shock caused by these orders before they were withdrawn and the concept of a mass attack abandoned. Following this only a few boats, sailing independently of each other, penetrated as far as the Brazilian coast.

The move into American waters had an advantageous knock-on effect in the French dockyards. Boats were longer at sea and generally sustained less damage than boats stationed in the eastern Atlantic. Repair gangs were able to turn them round faster than the time needed for crews to recover. In the German dockyards this efficiency was not matched. During the summer of 1942, more than four months were required for fitting out, causing a considerable delay in the numbers appearing at the front. This caused Dönitz to complain on 21 June, 'The poor situation in the building yards is now the most pressing problem of the war'.

Adding to the U-boat Command's difficulties was the almost total lack of intelligence support and, as a result, many problems were not recognised at the time. For example, sinkings by U-boats were over-estimated by up to 100 percent and Dönitz would probably have acted differently if he had known the true figures. The B-Dienst under KS Heinz Bonatz was a straightforward radio monitoring service. It supplied a mass of decrypted and translated signals, but did not have the staff to evaluate the contents and in that respect was different from the Royal Navy's Intelligence

Section. The fact that Germany did not have anyone keeping an eye on the overall proceedings made a significant contribution to the decision making processes. The small number of men at the U-boat Command, who were controlling the front lines, were often too engrossed in their battles to see things on a broader scale and in addition to this were located in France where they experienced all the limitations of living in a foreign and occupied country. The small staff worked under considerable stress for ten or more hours per day, often seven days a week and there was little time for individuals to look beyond their immediate operational tasks. They were encouraged to process information, but many details were overlooked because the men could not cope with the mass of paper on their desks. To make matters worse, much of this intelligence work had to be done after the completion of routine duties, when people were not perhaps at their best. One U-boat Command staff officer remembers, 'We were encouraged to consider intelligence matters. Everybody had a quick jab, whenever time allowed'. The terms U-boat Command and U-boat Arm tend to give the impression of a large organisation, but the reverse was true.

The picture painted by many historians of 1942 having been a successful year for U-boats does not tally with comments in war time diaries. The high level of merchant ship sinkings, due partly to the large number of U-boats at the front and also to the lack of opposition in American waters, concealed some worrying developments. For example, there was a steady decline in the performance of individual boats. The figure dropped from a peak in October 1940 of five and a half ships sunk per month per U-boat at sea, to an average of one and a half throughout the following year. For the first half of 1942 the numbers remained steady at about one and a half to two ships sunk per month per U-boat at sea. After September this total dropped to less than one. Dönitz became concerned with this lack of success and with the increasing difficulty that they were experiencing in locating convoys and in approaching them. He has been criticised by his own officers for running the U-boat Command in an obsessional way and for not taking adequate account of developments on the allied side. Some of his officers have suggested that he did not want to face up to the difficulties and to the soaring losses, and preferred to regard them as temporary episodes which would pass. Such comments would seem to be supported by remarks made by Dönitz throughout the autumn of 1942, but it should be remembered that these were made for consumption by the Supreme Naval Command and he probably used his penchant

A small coastal boat of Type IIB from the 21st U-Flotilla. Probably U24 under Helmut Hennig.

for the dramatic in order to galvanise his superiors into responding to his requests. Dönitz also made a number of public speeches and even a radio broadcast, but the gloom foretold in these can be disregarded as it was probably instigated by the government, possibly to prepare the German people for hard times ahead.

While the general situation for the war at sea looked bleak, there were still high hopes, in 1942, that a number of promising counter-measures would make some impact. Dönitz never had any illusions about winning the war at sea and during the autumn of 1942 his principal hope was that U-boats might play a role in helping to bring about a negotiated end to the hostilities. The U-boat Command had surmounted several major problems in the past and the following projects played a significant role in German decision making during September 1942:

1 The role of aircraft. The failure to develop a German Naval Air Arm is well known today. In 1942, the U-boat Command still had high hopes of receiving air support.

2 Anti-aircraft armament. Until this period of the war, U-boats had managed to avoid conflict by diving before weapons from the air could be brought to bear. Larger, faster flying aircraft made such evasion considerably more difficult and the first conning tower modifications, to strengthen anti-aircraft armament, went ahead during the summer of 1942. It was thought that this would make an immediate impact and at that time it was not known that another year had to pass before the larger guns would be ready for use at the front.

3 New torpedoes. Small warships, attacking U-boats at fast speeds became one of the most pressing problems of 1942. A special anti-destroyer torpedo, the so-called acoustic torpedo of Type Zaunkönig or G7s (better known as T5), was already developed and only awaiting manufacture. The first acoustic torpedo, a scaled

U1007, probably in Norway. KL Rolf Mützelburg (Commander of U203) was killed as a result of hitting his head on the saddle tanks during a dive from the top of the conning tower.

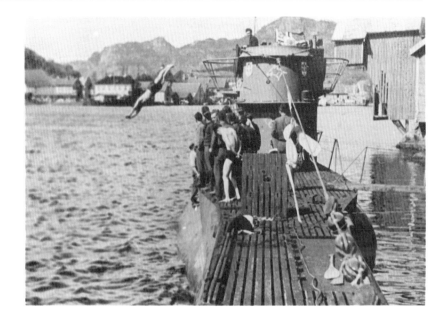

down version of the T5, was used during the spring of 1943, but it was not until the autumn of 1943 that the more effective T5 came into service. A long-range anti-convoy torpedo (FAT – Federapperat Torpedo and sometimes incorrectly called Flächenabsuch Torpedo) had been under development and, from the end of 1942 onwards, was manufactured at a rate of about 100 per month. Initial plans to restrict their use to radar equipped boats had to be abandoned because the electronic apparatus was not produced in sufficient numbers. The FAT, based on a G7a torpedo, travelled in a straight line for a pre-determined distance and then looped around in the hope of colliding with a ship in the convoy. The statistic of 806 torpedoes having been required to sink 404 ships was one of the most pressing reasons for this new introduction and, in the summer of 1942, the U-boat Command had high hopes of greatly improving efficiency with this new weapon; and the fact that a U-boat would not have to creep in close to a convoy was another point in its favour.

4 Radar and radar detection equipment. Having realised radar played such a major role, the German High Command thought the escorts' superiority could be neutralised by equipping boats with radar detection aids.

5 In the long term Dönitz was staking high hopes on the highly futuristic boats and torpedoes with Walter turbines.

13. The Return to Mid-Atlantic

U-boats heading towards United States waters usually travelled at economical cruising speeds along routes not frequented by the enemy. This policy was changed during May 1942, when a group, identified by the name HECHT, made the crossing along tracks where merchant ships might be expected. Five convoys were found, more than had been anticipated, and this, together with the increasing number of new boats coming to the front, prompted U-boat Command to prepare for a resumption of attacks in the air gap of the mid-Atlantic. Indeed, Dönitz had little choice. Following the evacuation of the Atlantic during the previous November, U-boats focused on Gibraltar where they experienced strong opposition and Dönitz was not happy with the thought of striking at convoys within range of air and surface support from the Rock. Germany did want to provoke the still neutral countries in southern America, and so the western side of the South Atlantic was out of bounds and only a limited number of opportunities remained in the United States for a small number of U-boats. So, Dönitz had the choice of either going into African waters or returning to the convoy routes between America and Britain. Increased air cover from British, Icelandic and Canadian bases limited operations in the North Atlantic to the now narrow air gap of the middle, where U-boats could still expect to operate for short periods without interference from other air cover.

June to November 1942

The long journeys to the attack areas in United States waters had already made it impractical to give each boat detailed instructions because such information was invariably out of date by the time commanders were supposed to act upon it. Therefore, boats sailed with orders to make for a specific area and then await further details on arrival. As a result, a huge mass of information was broadcast from U-boat Command, and the Operational Intelligence Centre of the Royal Navy had a field day. Although Bletchley Park, the British decyphering centre, did not succeed in breaking into the new German radio code (which had been introduced at the beginning of 1942) until the end of that year, Rodger Winn's (head of the secret submarine tracking room at Admiralty in London) revolutionary hypothesis of forecasting U-boat movements was now paying dividends. Having recognised the attack patterns he was able to

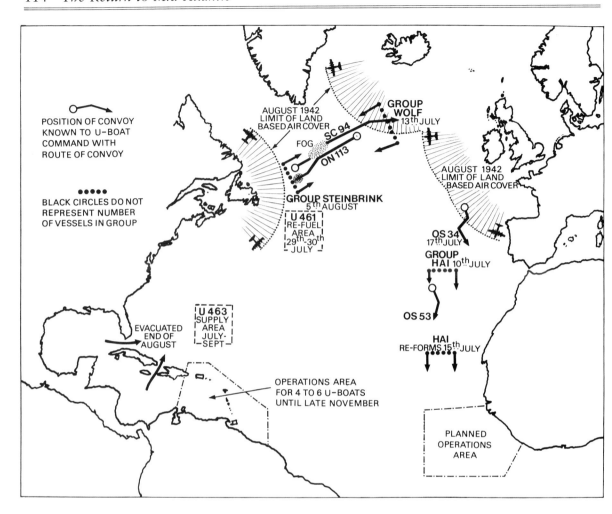

U-boat operations: July to August 1942.

Group STEINBRINK versus convoy SC94		
U71	OL	Hardo Rodler von Roithberg
U210	KL	Rudolf Lamcke
U379	KL	Paul-Hugo Kettner
U454	KL	Burkhard Hackländer
U593	KL	Gerd Kelbling
U597	KL	Eberhard Bopst·
U607	KL	Ernst Mengersen
U704	KL	Horst Kessler
U461	KK	Wolf Stiebler
U463	KK	Leo Wolfbauer

Group WOLF		
U43	OL	Hans-Joachim Schwantke
U71	OL	Hardo Rodler von Roithberg
U86	KL	Walter Schug
U90	KL	Hans-Jürgen Oldörp
U379	KL	Paul-Hugo Kettner
U454	KL	Burkhard Hackländer
U552	KK	Erich Topp
U597	KL	Eberhard Bopst
U607	KL	Ernst Mengersen
U704	KL	Horst Kessler

The narrow upper foredeck of U405 with men working near the torpedo storage container, trying to get at their inflatable dinghy, which was stored next to it.

Left: U405 (KK Rolf Heinrich Hopman), with a polar bear insignia on the tower and an iceberg in the background, while pursuing convoy PQ18 in northern latitudes. The thick, forward jumping wire served as a means of securing harnesses for men working on deck and as radio aerial. The connection to the conning tower socket can clearly be seen.

gain some useful information from the nature of the signals even though the exact content remained a mystery.

The first North Atlantic wolf pack to assemble after the withdrawal of November 1941, identified as Group WOLF, was established some 500 miles west of North Channel on 13 July 1942. The plans were for the group to remain in the air gap with a U-tanker (U461, KK Wolf Stiebler) for as long as possible. This operation further emphasised the widening rift between Dönitz and the Supreme Naval Command, which was not informed about Group WOLF and reacted rather caustically when details were discovered. The distance between Dönitz in Paris and his superiors in Berlin helped lighten the effects of their strong objections to his secretive ways of working. Dönitz did not appear to be easily ruffled at protestations from his superiors and in May 1942 was far more concerned at finding means of receiving up-to-date information from the front. In this respect, the summer of 1942 saw an innovation in communication, the so-called Funkschlüsselgespräch (Radio Code Conversation). This had been pioneered earlier in the spring by KK Waldemar Seidel (Commander of the Naval Arsenal in Lorient) in the radio station at Kerneval and Funkmeister Wolfgang Hirschfeld in U109 (KL Ajax Bleichrodt), which was docked in

Group LOHS versus convoys SC94, SC97 and ON129

U135	KL	Friedrich-Hermann Praetorius
U174	FK	Ulrich Thilo
U176	KK	Reiner Dierksen
U256	KL	Odo Loewe
U373	KL	Paul-Karl Loeser
U432	KL	Heinz-Otto Schultze
U438	KL	Rudolf Franzius
U569	KL	Hans-Peter Hinsch
U596	KL	Gunter Jahn
U605	KL	Herbert-Viktor Schütze
U660	KL	Götz Baur
U705	KL	Karl-Horst Horn
U755	KL	Walter Göing
U461	KK	Wolf Stiebler
U462	OL	Bruno Vowe

Group VORWARTS

U91	KL	Heinz Walkerling
U92	KL	Adolf Oelrich
U211	KL	Karl Hause
U407	KL	Ernst-Ulrich Brüller
U409	OL	Hans-Ferdinand Massmann
U411	OL	Gerhard Litterscheid
U604	KL	Horst Höltring
U609	KL	Klaus Rudloff
U659	KL	Hans Stock
U756	KL	Klaus Harney

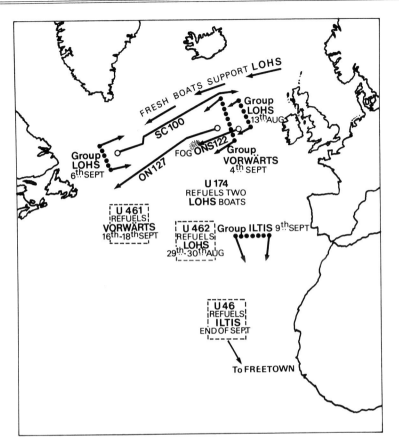

U-boat operations: August to September 1942.

Lorient. The first operational call was made on 25 July, when Dönitz called KL Erich Topp in U552. Using the telephone on his desk, Dönitz dictated a message to a code writer operator and the morse signal was transmitted for the U-boat the moment the letter was illuminated above the keyboard. This lengthy process – it took 75 minutes to pass over some 18 lines of typewritten text – meant it could only be used after an action, when the location of the U-boat was known to the Allies. Following the radio conversation with Topp, Dönitz remarked that the new technique, although lengthy, proved to be an excellent means of getting up-to-date news from the front.

Bad weather prevented a serious attack by boats from Group WOLF against convoy ON113 during mid July 1942 and gave Britain a breathing space to play the next major card. More

U563 coming alongside another boat.

land-based aircraft were deployed in the air gap to reduce its size, and though it was not closed completely, air support now extended some 800 miles from allied bases. As a result, the inexperienced boats of Group STEINBRINK found it almost impossible to maintain contact with their targets when they tried to track convoys SC94 and ON115 towards the end of July 1942. Some of the boats were attacked at hourly intervals during daylight and were unable to remain on the surface long enough to move into favourable attacking positions for the night. Nevertheless, despite this most unwelcome opposition, 11 ships were sunk, though three U-boats were lost in exchange and seven more were damaged. In summarising Group STEINBRINK'S operation against Convoy SC94 Dönitz pointed out that the highly variable visibility presented opportunities for surprise attacks from aircraft. Several boats were approached at such fast speeds that they did not have sufficient time for diving. Such losses could not be sustained, but the decisive point was that so many boats managed to get within shooting range, in face of such strong opposition. He emphasised that all boats, except U607 (KL Ernst Mengersen), had inexperienced commanders, who were working in poor weather conditions, and that there were a number of torpedo failures. Dönitz thought that these were probably due to inexperience and caused by men not carrying out the correct procedure in the heat of battle. These failures were by no means isolated cases. In other actions, U130 (KL Ernst Kals), for instance, had a complete salvo fail against *Empress of Canada* and U84 (KL Horst Uphoff) reported failures during early August, but it was mid September before the U-boat Command recognised the scale of the problem.

While assessing the operations of July and August 1942, Dönitz recognised that the difficult situation at sea meant that only older and more experienced commanders managed to get close enough to targets to shoot. Yet despite this, he said that it would be necessary to send younger and less skilled men into the conflict. He concluded his summary by saying, 'There is no way of getting around the fact that the higher skills of convoy attacks cannot be taught at home, but must be learnt by facing the enemy'. This statement seems to underline a fundamental difference between the German and British navies. Earlier in the war, Dönitz had regarded training as vitally important and he often emphasised the high quality of the comprehensive prewar education programmes. Yet now, after the war had been in progress for almost three years, men received only a brief training of around three to five months and were then sent out to face the enemy. This approach was different to the Royal Navy inasmuch as the majority of anti-submarine forces started the war with little training, but received more as the war went on.

*   *   *

While Group STEINBRINK's attack on convoy SC94 was being analysed a number of setbacks occurred. U166 (KK Hans Günther Kuhlmann) was lost in the Gulf of Mexico, shortly after a successful mine-laying mission in the Mississippi Delta. Two boats located in the Caribbean, U94 (OL Otto Ites) and U654 (OL Ludwig Forster), were also sunk, which demonstrated that even the western and remoter parts of the Atlantic were proving hostile. KK Harro Schacht (U507), fed up with patrolling the apparently empty seas around St Paul's Rock, was granted his request to penetrate into Brazilian waters. In addition to this activity on the western side of the Atlantic, six boats of Group HAI had gone south to start a patrol line to the west of Cape Finisterre and continued as far as Sierra Leone in Africa before finally dispersing towards the end of July.

The next major strike into the South Atlantic, with Group EISBÄR sailing during early August, provoked a considerable exchange of strong words between Dönitz and the Supreme Naval Command. The Naval Command ordered U-boats south from the earlier operations areas around Freetown, into a zone which had in 1940 and 1941 been the exclusive domain of surface raiders, but prohibited attacks en route. The argument put forward was that any U-boat attacks would alert the Allies and so hinder the chances of surprise further south. Dönitz argued that it would be better to sink shipping as close to home as possible. 'What is the point of going half way around the world to Cape Town, if we can achieve the same results by only just crossing the Equator? U-boats have operated as far as St Helena before and there are no reasons why further sinkings there should lead the enemy to conclude a strike against South Africa is underway. Strategic pressures alone do not warrant boats going that far. Four boats (U68 KK Karl-Friedrich Merten, U156 KK Werner Hartenstein, U172 KL Carl Emmermann and U504 KK Fritz Poske) as well as a supply boat (U459 KK Georg von Wilamowitz-Möllendorf) will be tied up for a considerable time of possibly more than six months, making any cut in such a long undertaking more than welcome.'

U172, under KK Carl Emmermann, showing the upper deck heads.

The outcome of this thrust into far southern waters is well known today. Several books have been written about the incident in which U156 sunk the liner *Laconia* with over a thousand Italian prisoners of war on board. An attack against overloaded U-boats and lifeboats during a German rescue attempt led Dönitz to order, 'All attempts at rescuing survivors are to be stopped. Such action contradicts the necessity of war and hard decisions must be taken. Survivors are only to be picked up if they are commanding officers, engineering officers or if they are required for questioning. Remember the enemy is bombing German cities without regard for women and children'.

The next four North Atlantic convoy attacks, towards the end of August 1942, were disappointing for the U-boat Command. Group LOHS was sent against convoys SC97 and ON127, and the remaining boats then sailed with Group VORWÄRTS against SC99 and ON129. A remarkable feat was achieved by the boat furthest away from these convoys, U660 (KL Götz Baur), which travelled continuously for almost two days at top speed to come close to the merchant ships, but bad weather prevented it from getting within shooting range. Weather also played a decisive role in other battles. Thick fog came down at dusk just at the critical moment when nine boats were getting ready to begin running in on convoy SC94. Consequently, many lost touch with their quarry and, to make matters worse, some of them came under heavy artillery attack in the thick fog, confirming that escorts were equipped with highly effective radar. Dönitz remarked that, despite having invested in improved sound detection gear to help locate convoys, U-boats were at considerable disadvantage without radar and radar detectors. The great length of the patrol lines, stretching over distances of 300 nautical miles (550 km), and the fact that the convoys were about that distance apart, added to the Germans' problems.

Despite the poor results, Dönitz remained quite optimistic, saying, 'Convoy attacks are still possible as long as there is no air cover and we have sufficient boats in the patrol formation. Seventy-five percent of the commanders were on their first operation and they still managed to keep contact with the heavily defended convoys'.

Following the successes of Group HECHT in May, Dönitz said there had been no significant changes in the convoy war since the evacuation of the North Atlantic during the previous November. This opinion was modified throughout the summer of 1942 and on 2 October 1942 he told the Supreme Naval Command that the significant increase in the numbers of escorts was making it necessary for U-boats to take on convoy defences. Consequently, the new anti-destroyer torpedo was urgently required. Fast escorts had so far not been primary targets simply because the small numbers had been easily avoided and anyway it was thought more profitable to reserve torpedoes for merchant ships. The strong opposition from escorts was partly a result of Britain's inability to break the new German code, which had been introduced at the beginning of the year. Although capable of estimating the number of U-boats on patrol, it had not always been possible to determine where they were. Thus it was difficult for convoys to avoid patrol lines as they had done during the latter part of the previous year. As a result, merchant shipping had to rely on stronger protection. This increase in the numbers of escorts, combined with the Allies' increasing familiarity with U-boat strategy and the use of improved technology, made it considerably more difficult for U-boats to shadow their targets. Dönitz told the Supreme Naval Command, 'This new threat can only be neutralised by increasing the number of U-boats. It has also been discovered that convoys are travelling along a greater number of varying routes, which means we need longer patrol lines with more boats'.

Two weeks later, in mid October, Dönitz emphasised the role of enemy radio detection by saying, 'It has become obvious that the enemy's excellent use of radar has made it impossible for U-boats to keep in contact with convoys. Recent successes by U607 (KL Ernst

U460, a supply boat of Type XIV, commissioned by KL Friedrich Schäfer and later commanded by KL Ebe Schnoor, supplying fuel in heavy North Atlantic weather.

Mengersen), U618 (KL Kurt Baberg) and U221 (KL Hans Trojer) were achieved during periods of bad weather, when enemy radar probably has little effect'.

The return of operations to the mid-North Atlantic brought with it several other problems, one of which involved the fuel consumption of the medium-sized U-boats like the Type VIIC. During the earlier American operations U-boats would travel across the Atlantic at their most economical cruising speed, intercept and attack merchant ships, and then cruise home. Operations against Atlantic convoys, on the other hand, required rather different strategy. Chasing convoys at high speed used up considerably more fuel and if U-boats were to attack convoys on both their outward and return journeys they would need to refuel from a supply vessel in mid-Atlantic.

At around this time, however, there appears to have been a difference of opinion regarding the usefulness of supply boats. On 2 October, Dönitz told the Supreme Naval Command that the presence of submarine tankers had greatly improved the performances of the smaller Type VII boats, but this view was not shared by all his staff, or the commanders at sea, who were able to quote several cases of boats drifting for days on end without power for heating, lighting or cooking, before calmer weather allowed fuel to be transferred by rubber dinghy in 20-litre cans. Men at sea certainly noticed a considerable difference between refuelling off Bermuda during the spring and summer and doing the same off Iceland in autumn. In fact, weather played a crucial role throughout the convoy battles during the autumn of 1942. The seasonal gales set in early and raged with a severity that made it virtually impossible for the majority of boats to keep in contact with convoys.

In addition to operations in the air gap of the mid-Atlantic, the autumn of 1942 also saw activity in other areas. In September, U517 (KL Wolfgang Schultze) and U165 (KK Eberhard Hoffmann) located heavy traffic in the Gulf of St Lawrence and, in October, another group was sent there. However, the three boats, U522 (KL Herbert Schneider), U521 (KL Klaus Bargsten) and U520 (KL Volkmar Schwarzkopf) found the hunting grounds empty and KL Friedrich-Wilhelm Wissmann's (U518) departure from the New-foundland Bank in early November marked the temporary aban-donment of Canadian waters.

Three boats, U126 (KL Ernst Bauer), U161 (KL Albrecht Achil-les) and U159 (KL Helmut Witte), were sent to the Congo estuary where it was thought that a high concentration of merchant ships might be found. It did not materialise, however, and the last mentioned boat was diverted to Cape Town, where equally lean conditions were experienced. The western zone of the Atlantic was still regarded unfavourably, though a group of four U-boats made for the Lesser Antilles. The end of November saw the longest chase for a single freighter when U176 (KK Reiner Dierksen) pursued the 5922 GRT *Polydorous* for two days in the St Paul's Rock area.

Operation Torch, the allied landings in North Africa during November 1942, could hardly have been prevented by U-boats. Indeed, any intervention at the time when the Allies were estab-lishing beach-heads would have proved costly, and though the U-boat Command was aware of an increase in activity around Gibraltar they avoided the waters, principally as a result of their unhappy experiences there at the beginning of the year. The Sup-reme Naval Command did not send any directives about the allied landings and those boats which were eventually sent south, arrived after the initial hubbub had died down. It is worth mentioning, as a footnote, the unintentional help the allied offensive was given by U-boats. An attack on convoy SL125 by Group STREITAXT lasted for five days and drew U-boats away from the routes along which the allied invasion ships were travelling.

14. Resignations and Promotions

1943 began with two remarkable resignations and an even more extraordinary promotion. Heinrich, better known as Ajax, Bleichrodt (U109), one of the outstanding U-boat commanders and holder of the Oakleaves to the Knights Cross, relayed back to U-boat Command over the radio his refusal to continue fighting. At about the same time, Grand Admiral Erich Raeder (Supreme Commander-in-Chief of the Navy) offered his resignation in private. In retrospect, Dönitz's subsequent promotion to this top post may appear to have been the obvious move, but at the time it seemed extraordinary simply because he had hardly ever been inside the Supreme Naval Command, and he lacked the usual experience and qualifications for the position.

An accident had caused Bleichrodt to join the navy. He was an officer cadet in the merchant marine when the sail training ship *Niobe* went down in the Fehmarn Belt, taking with her almost an entire year's (1932) intake of naval officers. To try to replace these losses, Raeder wrote to Germany's leading shipping firms, asking their best men to come forward as replacements. Bleichrodt joined U-boats late in 1939, after serving aboard the battlecruiser *Admiral Hipper* and, being exceptionally talented, went straight in to command U48, without passing through the watch officer roles. Two and a half years of uninterrupted action then took its toll. Parts of his last voyage in U109 are well documented and several historians have commented upon the boat's empty handed return, though Bleichrodt had in fact been to the shores of South America rather than in the convoy routes of the mid-Atlantic, as some have assumed. On reaching Cayenne in French Guiana, he sent a message, 'For the past ten days commander has been suffering from nervous weaknesses, emotional despondency and loss of energy. Request permission to go home'. This arrived during the early hours of 27 December 1942, some time after Dönitz had gone to bed. No one on duty was unduly perturbed and the Commander-in-Chief saw it when he came into the office in the morning.

Bleichrodt began his career in U48 because a particularly difficult crew needed a 'tough nut' to control them. Earlier, while in the Bay of Biscay, he was ordered to break off his passage across the Atlantic to seek out the British commando force which had

Dönitz and KK Georg Schewe, who commanded U60, U105 and later became U-boat Flag Officer. The badges on the jacket are from top to bottom: U-boat Badge of World War II, Clasp to the Iron Cross of 1914, the Iron Cross of 1939 and the U-boat Badge of World War I.

Dönitz shaking hands with KL Otto Stroeffler of U475 while greeting the crew after their second operational tour towards the end of 1943. The baton in his left hand is the Interimstab, which was made of ebony with silver and perhaps gold decorations at the top. Dönitz sometimes carried another plainer ebony stick of similar length but with a small silver knob at the top.

Obermaat Albert Jungclaus of U377 with magnetic compass attached to the attack periscope mount. The sighting device on the top was removable and only attached when required.

mounted the famous raid on St Nazaire, but Bleichrodt argued that anyone smart enough to launch such an attack would not hang around for punishment from a U-boat. He thus ignored the order and continued on his voyage. A few weeks later, while operating off America, he was repeatedly asked, and finally ordered, to broadcast his position. Much later, long after the U-boat Command had assumed U109 to be sunk, there came the signal, 'From U109 to BDU. No targets. Temperatures unpleasant. Request permission for an excursion to Bermuda'.

The signal Dönitz found on his desk in the morning of 27 December appeared more serious and a forceful message was sent to remind Bleichrodt who was boss: 'BDU to U109. Operation must continue under all circumstances'. Four days later, on the morning of New Year's Day, Dönitz was faced with, 'Bleichrodt to BDU. I am not fully operational at the moment. Please send medical advice'. A short time later, the reply went off, 'BDU to Bleichrodt. Continue with your operation. If necessary hand over command with full responsibility to first officer. Doctor suggests you take luminalette [a drug used to calm the nerves and induce sleep] three times a day'.

It did not work. Bleichrodt may well have been at his wits' end, but his hard, stubborn self was not broken. He refused to pass the burden of command to another person, who was in no position to refuse it, and the following day he sent a short signal: 'U109 to BDU. Have commenced return voyage due to shortage of fuel'.

The torpedoes of U109 were later handed over to boats of the Group DELPHIN, who had expended theirs against tankers of convoy TM1. On arrival in France, Bleichrodt was quietly removed from the scene, given a brief holiday and then pushed into an education unit. However, men of his high calibre were becoming rare and it was not long before he was back in action as chief of the 22nd Training Flotilla.

Grand Admiral Erich Raeder's resignation in January 1943 had rather more serious consequences. Though Raeder was almost 67 years old and had served as Supreme Commander-in-Chief of the Navy for just over 14 years, no one had been especially prepared to step into his shoes. Both his immediate predecessors, Paul Behnke (appointed 1920) and Hans Zenker (appointed 1924) were 54 years old when they took command and each remained in the post for four years. In view of Raeder's age and length of service, it might have been expected that the Naval Command would have had deputies in the running for this high office. Raeder nominated the 58-year-old Admiral Rolf Carls (Commander-in-Chief of Naval Group Command North) as his most suitable successor, but also suggested Dönitz to Hitler should the Führer have wished to emphasise the importance of the U-boat war.

Dönitz's appointment was a great personal triumph and a boost to the morale of the U-boat arm, but there were some distinct disadvantages involved in it. Though in retrospect the promotion appears to have been the right one, it did remove the brains of the U-boat campaign from the operations room, and reduce the already overworked staff by one. The earlier spy hunts had decreased the numbers to an absolute minimum and it was difficult to fill the sudden vacuum; particularly as the men who might take on the task were as mentally tired as Bleichrodt, having toiled under high strain and for long hours in the same job for a number of years.

Dönitz, who had never been trained as a staff officer, was not familiar with the delicate intricacies of the Naval Command and, in addition, had been incarcerated within the narrow confines of the U-boat operations room for eight years. During that time he had had several major disagreements with the departments he was now to command. To make matters worse, he took over Raeder's role at the most difficult stage of the war. All fronts were falling: the battle in the Atlantic had been lost; whole armies had been sacrificed in Russia; the Battle of Stalingrad had been fought and lost; the North

Hermann Patzke, Zentralemaat of U377 (KL Otto Köhler), wearing the type of U-boat overalls which were based on British battle dress. His rank, Maat, is indicated by collar patches. On his left pocket are the U-boat and Minesweeper badges. The last-mentioned was also awarded for other so-called security activities. Hermann Patzke served his naval apprenticeship aboard the state yacht, Grille.

African Campaign was in full retreat, and the naval leadership had no option other than to become fully involved in political struggles.

Dönitz took the new post of Supreme Commander-in-Chief of the Navy while at the same time keeping his old title of Commander-in-Chief of U-boats. Admiral Hans-Georg von Friedeburg, who had been chief of the Organisation Department, which included everything to do with U-boats except operational control, now delegated much of his work to enable him to take on a bigger role in the running of what had already been described as 'the Fourth Branch of the Armed Forces (ie, Army, Air Force, Navy and U-boats). Kpt. z. S. Eberhard Godt, Dönitz's number one in the operations department, was promoted to Konteradmiral and took greater control in the job he had been doing since the beginning of the war.

While most of the daily routine was delegated to these capable hands, assisted by a number of experienced ex U-boat commanders, Dönitz tried to reorganise the top-heavy naval administration and keep his hand on the pulse of the war. In the rapidly changing circumstances, he tried to find a new role for the navy, and he acted as liaison officer between Hitler and the Naval Command; he also attempted to find ways of improving the U-boats' performances. His promotion on 30 January 1943, the 10th Anniversary of the NSDAP coming to power, was followed by the U-boat Command's move from Paris to Berlin. Faced with the choice between Paris and Berlin, Dönitz chose the latter. Unlike his predecessor, he considered it important to be in close touch with Hitler's headquarters. The entire U-boat Command, small enough to be accommodated in several cars and with only their radio transmitter requiring a small lorry, was easily moved. The staff was housed in a hotel at Steinplatz (Charlottenburg) until better accommodation was provided inside a purpose-built bunker, code named Koralle, some 30 km from the Reichschancellery near the small village of Bernau.

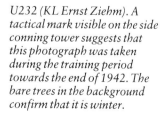

U232 (KL Ernst Ziehm). A tactical mark visible on the side conning tower suggests that this photograph was taken during the training period towards the end of 1942. The bare trees in the background confirm that it is winter.

U109 returning to port with Ajax (Heinrich) Bleichrodt on the right. Bleichrodt did not believe in wasting good clothes and, when at sea, usually wore his oldest garments. Behind him is a 20mm anti-aircraft gun.

There had also been a significant promotion on the other side of the Channel. In November 1942, Admiral Sir Max Horton (Flag Officer for Submarines) succeeded Admiral Sir Percy Noble as Commander-in-Chief of the Western Approaches. His place at HMS *Dolphin* in Gosport was taken by Rear Admiral (Act) C B Barry. Percy Noble had taken office in Liverpool during February 1941, at the same time as the U-boats' First Happy Time was coming to an end, and the following months witnessed immense changes in the war against U-boats. His successes cannot be gauged by the number of U-boats sunk because there were not enough escorts to hunt them to extinction. Instead, the Royal Navy had to concentrate on keeping attackers at bay. The effectiveness of individual U-boats certainly declined from October 1940 onwards and a considerable part of this success must be attributed to the new methods introduced by Sir Percy Noble. In November 1942, he was promoted to head of the Royal Navy Mission in the United States, where he also acted as the First Sea Lord's Washington Representative. Finding a successor to take over the Western Approaches was not easy and Max Horton was chosen because of his outstanding record as a submarine commander in World War I and his success as Flag Officer in World War II. In addition, he had a good understanding of both the technical and human problems faced by U-boats.

15. First Problems as Supreme Commander-in-Chief

January to March 1943 It has been suggested in some quarters that when Dönitz accepted the position of Supreme Commander-in-Chief of the Navy, he still had hopes that Germany might win the war. This is far from the truth. He did not even have such illusions at the beginning of the war and he took on the new challenge principally in the hope of being able to negotiate peace with the Allies on terms better than the unconditional surrender which they were demanding.

To this end, one of Dönitz's first steps as Supreme Commander-in-Chief of the Navy was to formulate a new naval policy. The old one, centred around the employment of capital ships, was desperately out-of-date. The general situation suggested that capital ships would be destroyed fighting pointless and bloody battles without contributing to the war effort. In World War I big ships did not have the range to operate far from base and now they lacked the technology to face the enemy. Yet, despite this outlook, Dönitz did not agree with Hitler's decision to scrap them. He argued that they still consumed considerable enemy resources, which could be thrown against other targets once it was realised they were no longer a threat. The U-boat war was Germany's only means of applying limited pressure and Dönitz felt the campaign had to continue, and with greater vigour, although at the same time he acknowledged Britain's and America's superiority in the Atlantic.

After U-boats, the second line of attack was to come from a combination of aircraft, mines and large groups of motor torpedo boats, operating in the Channel partly under the protection of mobile land-based artillery. There were plans to mobilise a good number of reconnaissance aircraft, as well as other squadrons, equipped to attack with torpedoes, mines and gunfire, none of which ever materialised. The small groups of planes which did come under naval control hardly made a significant contribution to the outcome of the war. Motor torpedo boats, which were at the core of these plans, were given considerable thought and the need to employ modern craft in large numbers and provide concrete shelters for their bases was emphasised.

Attacks by British aircraft, ships and commando groups had already demonstrated Germany's problems of protecting a long coastline, stretching from Norway's North Cape to the Spanish

border in the south and continuing for a long distance along the Mediterranean shores. Dönitz put the building of minesweepers, destroyers, small patrol boats and *Sperrbrechers* high on the list of priorities. In addition to this, he supported the navy in its appeal for more and better fighter and anti-aircraft cover for vital target areas, especially for the ports which could easily be shut down by enemy action. One further priority was that the Baltic be kept clear of mines, to enable U-boat training to continue without interruption.

Neither Dönitz nor the U-boat Command had any illusions as to their power. The draft of the new policy contained calculations demonstrating that the quantities of steel and manpower required to meet the demands were impossible to achieve. However, it also pin-pointed areas for improvement. Many skilled men from the shipbuilding yards, for example, were still being called up for service with the armed forces and a plea was made to keep this expertise where it could be better used. As a result, Hitler re-classified building and repair yard workers.

Günter Hessler and Alfred Hoschatt have pointed out that the various setbacks of early 1943 were not recognised by the majority of German people and even top army leaders over-estimated Dönitz's capabilities. 'People respected him and had blind faith in his abilities.' A similar view is held by some historians, who have attributed super human qualities to this small Prussian naval officer

Dönitz greeting the crew of U475 (KL Otto Stroeffler). He is holding his Interimstab and behind him is his adjutant, KK Walter Lüdde-Neurath, whose position can be identified by the so-called 'Affenschaukel' (Monkey's Swing) on his right shoulder. There were no definite rules in the navy as to which salute should be used and both were acceptable, although the traditional military greeting was used more often than the party greeting.

KL Hubert Nordheimer commissioning U237 on 30 January 1943. The boat has already been fitted with a Type 1 conning tower modification which carried two single 20mm anti-aircraft guns. Heavier armament was not available until the summer of that year.

and forgotten that he took the job of Supreme Commander-in-Chief in the hope of being able to reach a negotiated peace.

Dönitz's promotion took place against the increased determination of the Allies to put an even higher priority on defeating the German Navy. At the Casablanca Conference it was made quite plain that an invasion of Europe could only be considered when the Allies controlled the vital supply routes in the Atlantic.

As early as the summer of 1940, the Admiralty and the Coastal Command of the Royal Air Force requested permission to bomb French U-boat bases and this pressure was intensified when details about the construction of the concrete U-boat pens became known. The combination of flimsy dams, foundations below sea level and the necessity of constant pumping to keep the sites dry, made them exceptionally vulnerable targets, but in the early stages of the war Britain showed little interest. The bombing of these sites was discussed again towards the end of 1942. The Air Staff still considered that the undertaking could not justify the bombing of French civilians. After the Casablanca Conference, this opinion changed and the British Cabinet approved the start of a new bombing offensive. The first raid, consisting of 100 bombers against Lorient, took place during the night of 14-15 January 1943. In the next three months over 3000 aircraft sorties were flown against French ports and 1800 against bases in Germany. Norwegian ports were also attacked. Almost 7000 tons of high explosive were dropped, devastating houses around U-boat pens and killing many civilians, but doing little to curtail the U-boat war. A few boats were slightly damaged but only one, U622 (KL Horst-Thilo Queck), was sunk. The boat was caught by bombs in front of the pens in Trondheim. On the whole though the bombing campaign caused very little damage until 1945, when production was slowed down, though not completely halted.

A considerable shake-up of the Supreme Naval Command followed Dönitz's appointment and some historians have considered this to have been a move to bring the navy, still working on high Prussian standards, in line with NSDAP thinking. Political discussions are beyond the scope of this book; suffice it to say that Dönitz considered the Naval Command to be top heavy, with some departments being duplicated, and he searched for ways to streamline administrative processes.

By January 1943, it was becoming clear that a new type of submarine, with considerably faster underwater speed, was going to be required to meet the changing opposition in the Atlantic convoy battles. It is now well known that a revolutionary new

The 88mm quick-firing gun of U405. Note that the gunsight is clipped in position on the left.

submarine, an 80-ton version of the Walter boat, had been launched in 1940, but the Naval Command had shown little interest in the craft. Concentrated and highly volatile hydrogen peroxide was injected into a closed circuit power plant to achieve a high underwater speed, without recourse to oxygen from the air. The subsequent evolution of this programme, as well as the development of the electro-submarine of Types XXI and XXIII, played no role in the outcome of the battles in the Atlantic and therefore the stories are beyond the scope of this book. However, it needs to be pointed out that the development of these submarines did consume a considerable proportion of available resources, and the German leadership hoped to use them, together with new weapons like the jet fighter, as a means of applying pressure so that the Allies might settle for a negotiated peace.

*   *   *

In February 1943, Dönitz was faced with the pressing problem of modifying existing submarine types to meet immediate demands. The following modifications came under consideration:

1 Increased anti-aircraft armament and removal of the 88mm and 105mm guns. New gun platform designs had been produced, but the 20mm quadruple and 37mm quick-firing guns were not yet ready. Consequently, a variety of different guns were mounted on the enlarged platforms. The first boat with this modification, U553 (KK Karl Thurmann), was sunk before conclusive tests could be made.

2 Radar detectors had been fitted as early as the summer of 1942, and the fragile wooden cross aerials were being replaced by circular dipole antennae which could be left on the conning tower when the boat dived.

3 The possibility of equipping boats with schnorkels, to enable diesel engines to be run under water, was discussed shortly after Dönitz became Supreme Commander-in-Chief of the Navy. The need for this equipment was not yet considered to be a high priority, but experiments went ahead.

4 Asdic foxers, already discussed in this book, had been under construction and Dönitz felt it was important to develop such equipment.

5 New torpedoes, one type to deal with fast-moving escorts and another for attacking convoys without having to approach too close, were in hand.

16. The Leadership has no Choice

There had been considerable U-boat activity in British coastal waters at the beginning of the war and spasmodic operations continued until the spring of 1941. By that time, most of the small Type II coastal submarines had joined training flotillas in the Baltic while the larger boats, under direct control of the U-boat Command, attempted to form patrol lines further out in the Atlantic. January 1943 saw a return to inshore waters with attempts made to operate off Land's End, in the Bristol Channel, off Peterhead in Scotland and at Scapa Flow in the Orkneys. U-boat Command records are somewhat unclear as they also list Plymouth but give the corresponding chart references as a location in the Bristol Channel. All boats destined to make for southwest England came from mid-Atlantic. A direct assault from the French bases was considered too risky. The Allies' detailed knowledge of U-boat positions was thought to be obtained by a combination of agents sending departure details and boats being tracked by a variety of methods based on radar.

January to February 1943

KK Otto von Bülow (U404) was some 450 km west of Ireland when he received a signal to open a sealed envelope in his safe. The instructions were short and clear: 'Make your way to Land's End and attack merchant shipping'. Details of minefields, estimates of convoy schedules, as well as a few tips and a message of encouragement were also enclosed. On 30 January, while heading east, U404 met up off southern Ireland with U333 (OL Werner Schwaff) and took delivery of some Asdic foxers. While von Bülow continued towards Cornwall at an economical cruising speed, KL Joachim Deecke (U584) excused himself from going into the Bristol Channel, on the grounds that a fault in his machinery made the boat too noisy. A day later, with the fault repaired, Deecke declared himself ready for the mission, but the task had already been handed over to U71 (OL Hardo Rodler von Roithberg). In the end, an alarming report from U404 caused the U-boat Command to cancel the special missions and both U584 and U71 remained in the Atlantic.

Von Bülow had planned to complete the last leg of his journey at speed, in order to approach the operations area and dive during the hours of darkness, but this did not work out. His radio operator received a number of signals from several land-based radar stations and the boat was attacked three times by aircraft with Leigh Lights. Evasive action caused the bow hydroplanes to be damaged on an underwater rock which in turn resulted in the batteries being quickly exhausted making any prolonged diving difficult. Having got north of Wolfe Rock and almost within sight of Land's End, von Bülow took the wise decision to abandon his objective and turned back into the open waters of the Atlantic.

In Bergen, two boats had been prepared for an assault on the north of Scotland. U376 (KL Friedrich-Karl Marks) was told to make for Peterhead and U377 (KL Otto Köhler) for Scapa Flow. Köhler was astounded by these instructions from the Commander of the 11th U-Flotilla (FK Hans Cohausz) and thought he was being sent on a suicide mission, but he and his men were in luck; despite the calm weather and reasonable visibility, they crossed the narrow seas without incident. But shortly before they came within sight of land their radar detector picked up signals and U377 had to be laid on the seabed to allow small boats in search formation to pass overhead. Shortly after surfacing, a destroyer approached on a collision course but U377 managed to avoid it. The day before U404 abandoned its mission off Land's End due to land-based radar Köhler sent a similar signal, saying he too was under threat from land-based radar. 'Submarines cannot be detected by radar over such long distances. The mission must continue,' came the reply.

This placed Köhler in a difficult predicament. First, he thought of what he had said shortly after commissioning U377 when he told his men, '. . . and above all I will do my best to bring you back alive'. Another man might have submitted to his superior's demands and accepted the statement that radar was not able to detect submarines over long distances. However, Köhler's mind also went back to the days when, as young naval officer, he had served in the communications department aboard the light cruiser *Königsberg*. He remembered how Germany's still primitive radar was used to show up marker buoys on both sides of the deepwater channels making it possible to negotiate hazardous waters during periods of bad visibility. During the autumn manoeuvres of 1938, when the U-boat staff used the cruiser as their headquarters, he took the opportunity to tell Dönitz about this invention, arguing that the device would be equally capable of detecting surfaced submarines. Dönitz showed no interest in *Königsberg*'s radar and, indeed, the idea was the cause of some ridicule amongst the assembled company. Now, in 1943, when he was faced with this most difficult

decision off Scapa Flow, he could clearly recall that indifference and ridicule. Being convinced that certain death was ahead of him, he ordered U377 to go the other way.

Köhler's remarks were not believed and Friedrich-Karl Marks was ordered to take over U377's objective. Though they had left Bergen together, U376 was some distance behind having lost the Obersteuermann (Navigating Boatswain) overboard. Following this loss, Marks had put into Hellesøy for a replacement. Despite the operations off Cornwall having been abandoned, and the mission of U377 aborted, Marks still sailed into the almost blinding radar impulses. Needless to say, he had no more luck than the other boats, but had the good fortune of being able to bring his boat home again.

U377 sailed around the north of Scotland, joined a patrol line for a brief period and then made for France, and arrived in Brest on 18 March 1943 to join the 9th U-Flotilla under KK Heinrich Lehmann-

A supply U-boat of Type XIV with a 37mm anti-aircraft gun forward of the conning tower.

The Biscay Cross radar detection aerial of U340 (OL Hans-Joachim Klaus). This had to be taken inside the boat before diving. The loop on the right is a radio direction detector, used for homing in on transmissions from other boats.

Willenbrock. Leaving his boat in Brest, Köhler travelled to Paris for a de-briefing before going on to Germany. The staff officers refused to believe in the intensity of radar signals and the interrogation ended in a roaring argument with Köhler being accused of lying. The argument then preceded him to Kiel when, on arrival, he was asked to give a report to Admiral Hans-Georg von Friedeburg, the 2nd Admiral U-boats and Commander-in-Chief of the U-boat Arm's Organisation Department. After Köhler told him his story and presented his arguments, von Friedeburg invited Köhler to join him for a walk. The two men strolled to the end of the Tirpitzmole, which served as the outer breakwater to the Kiel naval base and, with no risk of being overheard von Friedeburg told Köhler that he thought that his assumptions about radar were probably correct. He went on, 'But for goodness sake shut up and keep quiet or someone will lock you up. Take my word for it, we are in a difficult position, our leadership has no choice'.

17. The Ferocious Battles of Spring 1943

In March 1943, just as a wolf pack was ready to pounce, the fast HX229 eastward-bound convoy from Halifax ran into the slower SL122 convoy resulting in a concentration of almost 100 merchant ships. There followed the biggest convoy battle of the war which has often been singled out as representing the climax of the U-boat offensive. This is something of an over simplification and the serious loss of merchant shipping conceals the poor results achieved by individual U-boats. In October 1940, 66 ships were sunk while the daily average number of U-boats in the Atlantic was ten. In March 1943, the sinkings rose to 84 ships, but by then more than 100 U-boats were at sea.

The significant point about this incident is not that a large battle took place, but that it happened so late in the war. A dramatic increase in the number of U-boats had occurred as early as September 1942. The average number of U-boats in the Atlantic at any one time had risen from 25 in 1941 to about 50 during the first half of 1942. Then, from July onwards it increased rapidly to reach around 100 in September, and the number remained at this high peak until May 1943. These figures help to illustrate how well British anti-submarine measures had worked during 1942 and it is remarkable that the Royal Navy managed to fend off a big set-piece battle until March 1943. In short, Germany had 100 U-boats stationed in the Atlantic every day for seven consecutive months and yet failed to engage the enemy on any significant scale. Furthermore, Germany was made to pay a heavy price for what successes she did have. That U-boats failed to inflict heavier losses was due principally to the well developed defences of the convoys.

Before looking at the nature of the convoy battles of the first quarter of 1943 it is important to remember two points, which have already been mentioned. First, the long range of the new FAT torpedoes, which allowed them to be fired from well outside the convoys, combined with frequent interference from escorts, made it difficult to observe sinkings. Consequently, actual successes often amounted to less than half of those that were reported to the U-boat Command. At times this error was even worse and only one ship out of five, six or even seven attacked and believed sunk, actually went down. Commanders were well known for over-estimating their

U-boat operations: autumn 1943.

Group LEUTHEN

U229	OL	Robert Schetelig
U238	KL	Horst Hepp
U260	KL	Hubertus Purkhold
U270	KL	Paul-Friedrick Otto
U275	OL	Helmut Bork
U305	KL	Rudolf Bahr
U338	KL	Manfred Kinzel
U341	OL	Dietrich Epp
U377	OL	Gerhard Kluth
U378	KL	Erich Mäder
U386	OL	Fritz Albrecht
U402	KK	Siegfried, Freiherr von Forstner
U422	OL	Wolfgang Poeschel
U584	KL	Joachim Deecke
U641	KL	Horst Rendtel
U645	OL	Otto Ferro
U666	KL	Herbert Engel
U731	OL	Werner Techand
U758	KL	Helmut Manseck
U952	KL	Oskar Curio

Group ROSSBACH

U260	KL	Hubertus Purkhold
U275	OL	Helmut Bork
U279	KL	Otto Finke
U305	KL	Rudolf Bahr
U336	KL	Hans Hunger
U378	KL	Erich Mäder
U389	KL	Siegfried Heilmann
U402	KK	Siegfried, Freiherr von Forstner
U419	OL	Dietrich Giersberg
U448	OL	Helmut Dauter
U539	KL	Hans-Jürgen Lauterbach-Emden
U584	KL	Joachim Deecke
U603	OL	Rudolf Baltz
U631	OL	Jürgen Krüger
U641	KL	Horst Rendtel
U643	KL	Hans-Harald Speidel
U645	OL	Otto Ferro
U666	KL	Herbert Engel
U731	OL	Werner Techand
U758	KL	Helmut Manseck
U952	KL	Oskar Curio

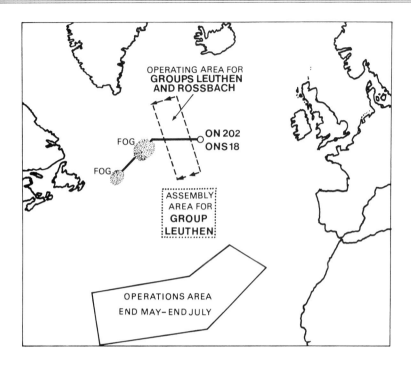

successes and the U-boat Command laundered the so-called *Schepke* or *Prien* tonnage to produce figures that were thought to be fairly accurate. However, from the autumn of 1942 onwards, it became more difficult to establish true success figures and Dönitz frequently based his reports on erroneous information. As has already been said, he might well have taken different decisions if he had been aware of the correct figures. The second significant point is that Britain managed again to break into the German radio code. The breakthrough came towards the end of 1942 after the vital parts of a new code writer had been captured from U559 (KL Hans Heidtmann) in October. Unfortunately, for allied merchantmen, the system was complicated and numerous blackouts were experienced throughout the first months of 1943. Some of the major U-boat successes can be attributed to such periods.

The improvement in convoy defences and the new pattern of the war which developed after the United States' entry into the conflict is illustrated by the massacre of convoy TM1 in January 1943. Seven out of nine tankers were sunk, representing the highest percentage loss of any convoy, and not a single U-boat was destroyed or seriously damaged. But, of the dozen U-boats involved, three failed to return because they were sunk elsewhere, another five went down during their next mission or shortly afterwards and two boats survived for another 12 months but only two saw the end of the war.

Convoy TM1, consisting of six tankers and three Flower class corvettes, left Trinidad for the Strait of Gibraltar on 28 December 1942. The destroyer *Havelock* followed with another three tankers, bringing the total up to nine by sunset of the following day. A Catalina of the western air cover attacked U124 (KL Johann Mohr) some 20 miles astern of this group after Mohr had taken a long-range shot at a lone tanker, but he was unaware of the convoy passing so close. He signalled U-boat Command to report no traffic and only meagre air cover. The secret submarine tracking room at the Admiralty in London breathed a sigh of relief as far as TM1 was concerned. The only obstacle in its path was the DELPHIN Group, some 900 nautical miles (1700 km) to the east but a safe distance north of TM1's route and known to be heading away from the danger area.

Unfortunately for the convoy, the tracking room did not know that KL Hans-Jürgen Auffermann (U514) had commenced his return journey from the Caribbean and he stumbled upon the tankers during the afternoon of 3 January 1943. On assessing his sighting report, Dönitz at first concluded that the convoy was too far away to be intercepted by the DELPHIN Group, though he fully appreciated the significance of the tankers making for Gibraltar which would be going on to support the African campaign. After further thought, he changed his mind and ordered all boats of DELPHIN Group plus U105 (KL Jürgen Nissen), which was some 450 km to the east, to intercept at fast cruising speed. Six hours later, the sighting by U182 (KL Nicolai Clausen) of convoy GUF3, heading west from Gibraltar to New York at 8 to 10 knots, persuaded U-boat Command to amend this order. DELPHIN Group was told to change course to pursue what was then identified as convoy number two, and it was calculated that the boats could still intercept TM1 if they missed GUF3.

Although Royal Navy intelligence failed to decypher U514's signal, the men in the tracking room guessed it was a U-boat's sighting report and direction finders located the source as near TM1. A change of course was ordered as soon as darkness offered some cover. *Havelock*, on the convoy's port bow, had just settled on the new heading when her Asdic gave warning of a submerged object 5000 yards (4500 metres) ahead. A radar response came shortly after an investigation had classified it as non-submarine and this was followed by a muffled explosion. It appears as if this

Boats remaining on operations in the Atlantic after 24 May 1943.

U91	KL	Heinz Hungerhausen
U202	KL	Günter Poser
U264	KL	Hartwig Looks
U304	OL	Heinz Koch
U378	KL	Erich Mäder
U413	KL	Gustav Poel
U418	OL	Gerhard Lange
U552	KL	Klaus Popp
U575	OL	Wolfgang Boehmer
U621	OL	Max Kruschka
U636	KL	Hans Hildebrandt
U645	OL	Otto Ferro
U650	OL	Ernst von Witzendorff
U664	OL	Adolf Graef
U731	OL	Werner Techand

The ace Adalbert Schnee on the left with the Chief of the 11th U-Flotilla, Hans Cohausz, who had earlier commanded UA and also became Chief of the Third Flotilla. The object to the left of Cohausz's nose is a heavily screened rear navigation light on the after edge of the conning tower.

confusion was due to *Havelock* picking up the U-boat a short time before it started surfacing. *British Vigilance* burst into flames, illuminating the surrounding sea as well as the perpetrator. *Empire Lytton*, the nearest ship to U514, reacted fast and, bringing her meagre armament to bear, went on a collision course. Several hundred small calibre shells hit the conning tower and the ramming attempt failed by only 20 yards, but put Auffermann off his objective who chose to dive deep. *British Vigilance*, although well ablaze, did not sink until three weeks later when U105 (KL Jürgen Nissen) finished off the abandoned wreck.

Though having shaken off U514, convoy TM1 was facing a number of pressing problems. Failure to supply the escorts with fuel during the previous day meant they were running low. Apparently, the escort commander (Commander R C Boyle) had not been correctly briefed before departure and tried the unrehearsed manoeuvre with the wrong tanker. This was aborted after considerable effort when it was discovered that *Norvik* did not carry the appropriate gear. Another attempt, this time with *Cliona*, during the morning of the next day, proved successful and all four warships were filled up. The second problem was caused by the escorts' direction finders. The convoy's only high frequency direction finder, fitted in *Havelock*, indicated a transmission ahead of the convoy during the morning of the fourth, when the first escorts were being refuelled. *Godetia* was sent ahead to investigate, but found nothing. Apparently, the source was over 100 miles ahead, which the HF/DF had failed to indicate. Then, shortly after this, the set lost power and finally gave out completely. *Godetia's* radar failed as well and *Pimpernel's* began to develop a defect which could not be repaired at sea. This left only *Saxifrage* and *Havelock* with serviceable radar equipment. The escorts had been in America for some time where a lack of spare parts had made it impossible to carry out all the necessary repairs. In addition to this, the ships had received a coat of grey paint, instead of the latest Atlantic camouflage, and this made them somewhat conspicuous.

Meanwhile, U182 (KL Nicolai Clausen), still following convoy number two (GUF3), was faced with determined opposition. Depth charges pushed the boat under and on resurfacing there was an immediate response from the radar detector, followed by a seven-hour depth charge hunt. At about the same time U575 (KL Günther Heydemann) sighted a convoy. The U-boat Command did not redirect DELPHIN Group towards it because if it was the same convoy as the one reported by U182, it meant that the merchant ships were travelling at about 15 knots, which was too fast for U-boats. If U575 had found a new convoy doing about 11 knots, it was futile to pursue it because all submarines were a considerable distance behind it. However, there followed a disagreement between Dönitz and his staff officers who were intent in pursuing U182's convoy. Dönitz argued that, although the exact position of TM1 was not known, tankers heading for the Mediterranean were more important than freighters going west. Overruling his men, he ordered DELPHIN Group into a north-south patrol line, to sail at seven knots and find TM1.

U381, almost at the northern end of the patrol line, sighted TM1 during the afternoon of 8 January and five boats, U571, U575, U442, U436 and U522, were in contact during the coming night. This produced a hive of activity on the air, but British naval intelligence was experiencing a temporary blackout and was unable to decypher the German signals. To make matters worse, Rodger

Winn, head of the secret submarine tracking room at the Admiralty in London and the person responsible for forecasting U-boat activities and instrumental in having prevented a recent major clash, had been on sick leave for four weeks prior to the battle for TM1. This absence, together with the failure of the only HF/DF in the convoy, meant TM1 continued on a course of 74 degrees at 9 knots. At 2100 hours, *Havelock* obtained a radar contact only 3200 yards away on the port bow and, on altering course, spotted a U-boat in the bright moonlight, but it vanished before a ramming attempt could be made. As *Havelock's* depth charges exploded, the tanker *Albert L Ellsworth* burst into flames. U436 (KL Günther Seibicke) had aimed at what appeared, to the first watch officer who was working the torpedo aimer, to be one target made up of three overlapping ships. The first of these, the commodore's ship *Oltenia II*, was broken in two, the second escaped undamaged and the third, *Albert L Ellsworth*, remained afloat in flames to be sunk by U436 during the next day. At the same time U575 approached but was intercepted before aim could be taken. Activity continued until shortly before 2200 hours, when *Havelock* fired star shells over another diving U-boat, but lost contact before depth charges could be thrown. The peace lasted for only one and a half hours, before *Pimpernel* forced U571 under. Again, contact was lost before depth charges could be released and the corvette did not waste much time before rejoining *Godetia* on the port wing of the convoy. U575 was in the process of shooting on 9 January just after midnight when further depth charges exploded. Whether these put the torpedoes off their target or whether they would have missed anyway will never be known, but nothing happened. A tense silence followed until 0500 hours when U522 (KL Herbert Schneider) torpedoed *Minister Wedel* and *Norvik*. *Saxifrage* and *Havelock* spotted a U-boat and chased it. It was not U522, however, but U381 (Count von Pückler und Limpurg). At the end of this chase, it was decided that *Havelock* should remain near the drifting wrecks to ambush the U-boat if it returned to finish off the tankers and the corvette rejoined the convoy. These plans to ambush submarines were quickly abandoned when Admiralty warned of six or seven U-boats near the convoy. *Havelock* made an unsuccessful attempt to sink the wrecked tankers with gunfire and then moved into station to help protect the remaining ships. It left *Norvik* in flames but *Minister Wedel* appeared to have suffered little damage. The fourth U-boat attack came shortly before 0630 hours when *Empire Lytton*, carrying highly volatile aviation fuel, was torpedoed by U442

The bows of a Type VIIC.

(KL Hans-Joachim Hesse). Shortly after this, U522 was attracted to the smoking remains of the two tankers abandoned by *Havelock* and sunk them.

At mid-day on the ninth, KL Rudolf Schendel (U134) found himself in front of the convoy when the hollow ping of an escort's Asdic was heard shortly before he prepared to take aim. *Godetia* was only 1800 yards (1600 metres) away and had just increased speed to 14 knots to explore the echo, when bubbles, caused by the passage of a G7a torpedo through the water, were spotted. Look-outs in *British Dominion* had seen the periscope on their starboard side and made an attempt to put Schendel off by shooting small calibre guns, but to no avail. A clearly defined bubble trail made for *Vanja*, but by prompt action she evaded its path. The men in U134 were in luck in that *Godetia* lost Asdic contact and could not pursue them with depth charges.

The rest of the day passed in peace. At dusk, the remains of the convoy were clearly silhouetted against the lighter western sky and men's nerves were strained to the limit with the sighting of a morse lamp on the dark eastern horizon in front of them. Night had fallen when *British Dominion* was hit by torpedoes fired from U522 (KL Herbert Schneider). As had happened before, the resulting fire illuminated the U-boat, and nearby ships were soon firing at it. Although the small calibre shells bounced off the conning tower, the response succeeded in driving off the attacker. Schneider had fired three times in close succession at a group of overlapping tankers and was under the impression he had sunk one and damaged another, but all three torpedoes had hit the same ship, *British Dominion*, which was later sunk by U620 (KL Heinz Stein). U571 (KL Helmuth Möhlmann) then came in to attack the remaining two tankers, *Vanja* and *Cliona*, but both escaped. At daybreak on 11 January, a Catalina from Gibraltar was spotted and the appearance of HMAS *Quiberon*, followed soon afterwards by the destroyers *Penn* and *Pathfinder*, was most welcome. The corvettes *Penstemon* and *Samphire*, together with the naval tug *Nimble*, were sent out to search for the abandoned wrecks along TM1's route, but U-boats had got there first and none was found. Dönitz guessed that the convoy had reached the air cover zone, where further attacks were futile, so he ordered the chase to be abandoned. A total of 15 ships of 141,000 GRT sunk is recorded in his war diary, but we know now that the true number was seven ships of 129,000 GRT.

Following the battle for the tanker convoy TM1, the stage was set for the massive attacks in March on convoys HX229 and SC122.

Though the bloody drama of this conflict has been fully described in many postwar books, it did not feature strongly at the time in the U-boat Command's records. But KA Eberhard Godt's (previously head of the U-boats' operations room and at this time head of the U-boat Command) evaluation of the actions taken by a small number of U-boats which had managed to find ways of avoiding enemy radar, is most interesting. To follow the chain of events leading to these remarks, it is necessary to go back to the last months of 1942, when there had been a dramatic change in the approach to attacking convoys.

The story started during the summer of 1942 with the fitting of the rough wooden cross-like aerials for detecting enemy airborne radar in the Bay of Biscay. At first, outward-bound boats handed the equipment, as well as the trained operator, over to homeward-bound boats, but later a few found their way into the Atlantic,

U97 (KL Hans-Georg Trox) on its way out of Pola, 5 June 1943, for its last operational tour. U97 had been in the Mediterranean since 1941. The seahorse, on the side of the conning tower, was put there while the boat was under the command of Udo Heilmann of Crew 33. The second commander (Friedrich Bürgel) belonged to the Olympia Crew of 1936 and added the rings, which had been adopted as Crew badge. U97's last commander (Trox) also belonged to the 36 Crew. The term 'Crew' was the German name for each yearly intake of officer candidates.

where they were put to good use for detecting the presence of aircraft around convoys. This resulted in the alarming discovery that radar was also being used by escorts, a discovery which was confirmed when boats reported being shelled by artillery during periods of poor visibility when they could not see their attackers. This was an uncomfortable turn of events for the Germans. Claims that radar was being used by the opposition had been rife throughout 1942 but each enquiry had discredited them. Instead, surprise attacks were blamed on such things as poor lookouts. In July 1942, following the first radio code conversation between Dönitz and KK Erich Topp in U552 everybody was satisfied that radar did not play a role in allied strategy. Less than two months later, U-boat Command was convinced that radar detectors were vital for further successes in the Atlantic.

Dönitz had just come to terms with the use of radar, and the first detectors were proving successful, when two important things happened in London. First, Britain managed to regain some insight into the German secret code and Rodger Winn (head of the secret submarine tracking room at the Admiralty) returned after four weeks' absence of sick leave. As a result, 1943 began with a number of convoys being routed away from wolf packs, and this was noticed by Konteradmiral Eberhard Godt who noted in the diary, 'It appears as if convoys are deliberately avoiding wolf packs'. The ink had hardly dried before this suspicion was confirmed by a surprise attack on the Italian submarine *Kalvi* while refuelling from U459 (KK Georg von Wilamowitz-Moellendorf) in a lonely part of the ocean, some 300 miles east of St Paul's Rock. Treachery was not ruled out, but the immediate reaction by officers of the U-boat Command was to point the finger at the radio code. However, after evaluating a number of similar incidents listed by Godt, the Communications Department of the Supreme Naval Command produced convincing evidence to suggest that the radio code had not been compromised. Instead, a net of aerial radar was thought to be responsible for plotting U-boat positions, although the experts hardly had the necessary data for making such assumptions. A few months earlier, presuming that British radio direction finders were responsible in tracking down positions, U-boats were ordered to restrict their broadcasts and Godt had no way of checking the Supreme Naval Command's suspicions until the boats in question returned to port and the commanders could be interrogated. By that time the incidents were often blurred, making it more difficult to draw definite conclusions.

The disastrous results of January 1943, when the majority of U-boats failed even to make contact with convoys, were followed by the introduction of a new technique. Up until January, commanders had orders to dive for about 30 minutes as soon as their radar warning devices produced a response. This had the disadvantage of allowing the convoy to gain four to seven miles and U-boats, when travelling on the surface, were often only three to five knots faster than convoys, making it difficult for them to sweep around the merchant ships for another attack from ahead. Early in February, commanders were told to evade the enemy by sailing on the surface at rightangles to a destroyer's approach as German radar experts pointed out to the U-boat Command that enemy radar lost contact with a target at about the same time as it appeared on the horizon. It was further suggested that wind washing over wave tops would produce enough clutter on enemy radar screens for U-boats not to be noticed.

U161 (KL Hans Lange) showing an enlarged conning tower to house additional anti-aircraft armament. This photograph, found in the U-boat Archive, was taken from the blockade breaker Pietro Orseolo. *This is the work of Heinz Tischer, who sailed with auxiliary cruiser* Thor. *Following the raider's destruction in Japan, Tischer returned to Europe aboard the blockade breaker, bringing with him a water-resistant box containing the films of* Thor's *epic voyage.*

The calm weather at the beginning of the hunt provided the next modification of these tactics. Some U-boats, once they had located the mastheads of escorts over the horizon, ran away at fast speed the moment they observed a change in course. This cat and mouse game appeared to work. After a while escorts lost interest, and this made it easier to approach closer without being pursued. Unfortunately, for the Germans, the idea that radar could not detect the small shape of a U-boat running away was misplaced. It was, in fact, the worsening weather which had made it more difficult for allied radar to detect U-boats. Dönitz appreciated the considerable strain such tactics put on the men, but used the successes as a lever to ask for still more U-boats. Six months earlier Dönitz had demanded a completely new breed of submarine and yet, in March 1943, when there were already over a hundred submarines at sea, he was asking for more of the older type.

As quickly as ideas were formulated for dealing with convoy defences so the Allies refined and improved their defences. There were several reports in March of boats having been attacked without any prior warning from their radar detectors. Initially, this was put down to equipment failure, lax lookouts or the enemy switching their radar sets off before starting their approach. Then two experienced U-boat commanders reported disturbing evidence of a new type of radar. KK Werner Hartenstein (U156) and KL Johann Mohr (U124) had radar detectors with a 'magic eye' to aid tuning and these devices indicated the presence of inaudible signals shortly before aircraft attacks. Neither of the two boats managed to return home, and the news worried both the U-boat Command and scientists working on the development of radar. The fears were further aggravated by people like Ali Cremer (U333), who was attacked by aircraft with Leigh Lights without warning and refused to accept his lookouts or radar operators were lax. Funkmaat Bruster of U214 (KL Günther Reeder) confirmed the 'magic eye' story by telling how his device made a slight movement, suggesting the set was receiving some inaudible signals. March 1943, the month which is usually regarded as the climax of the U-boat offensive, ended with intractable problems and the U-boat Command did not exactly know what to do next.

18.   Catastrophic Losses

The loss of so large a number of U-boats during May has resulted in that month being labelled as 'the turning point of the U-boat offensive'. Although U-boat sinkings did increase dramatically, there was no particular change of direction in the battle and all the factors which contributed to these losses had already made themselves felt. The U-boat offensive had been on the decline since March 1941 when Joachim Matz (U70), Günter Prien (U47), Otto Kretschmer (U99) and Joachim Schepke (U100) were sunk. Dönitz had been aware of the worsening situation as early as the summer of that year, but had thought that it was a passing phase, and the successes in American waters, during the first months the following year, prevented him from charting a defensive course until the situation came to a head in the summer of 1942. The losses of May 1943 were high and, Dönitz said that he was used to setbacks but he was not prepared for losses on the scale which were now encountered. Yet, although he reacted by withdrawing his forces from the North Atlantic, he did not regard the war at sea as totally lost and he retained his belief that U-boats remained unchallenged as the primary naval weapon until the very end of the war.

The events of the month of May have been described in many books and this chapter will make some attempt at analysing the reasons for the losses, but first it may be of interest to focus on one boat which survived the massacre. U377 (KL Otto Köhler) was in the Atlantic for the whole of May having been at sea since 14 April, and for most of that time was in the area where the majority of the losses occurred. Köhler devoted considerable time and energy to hunting convoys, but unknown to him, his navigator (Fähnrich zur See Fritz Beske) made an error in his calculations. Not wishing this to be exposed, Beske kept the mistake to himself and each day narrowed the difference between his figures and their true position until the two coincided. Today, it is well known how Britain decyphered German signals and how the secret submarine tracking room at the Admiralty used the locations broadcast by the Germans for directing their forces. So U377 probably survived simply because Beske's error made it impossible for allied forces to be directed to U377; instead, they would have looked some 100 miles from its real position. The error did not come to light until the first U377 reunion in 1982 when Beske told his story.

A whole range of varying factors contributed to the increase in U-boat losses and it is not easy to point the finger at any particular one. However the following were thought to have been crucial. First, there were the methods employed in training. In October 1940, Dönitz concluded a summary of a convoy battle by saying the successes were possible because the commanders and crews had gone through thorough prewar training programmes. Recognising this as the key to success, he added, 'The decisive point is always going to be the ability of the commander'. Less than a year later he had modified his thoughts, stating, 'The difficult conditions under which young commanders are working makes it necessary to constantly send advice. The three weeks of tactical training are not sufficient for the men to learn all the points taught in the two-year-long prewar course'. The deficiencies were overcome by sending advice to commanders at sea and, at times it would seem as if U-boats were in constant radio contact with headquarters. Indeed the whole approach to the U-boat war changed from commanders being free to make their own decisions at sea to them being ordered, over the radio, as to what to do. There were even cases of commanders being prevented from attacking targets they had sighted because the persons around the green table in the control room on land suggested it might be better to pursue a different goal.

The lack of training led to many elementary mistakes being made. Working as a team, men were often able to cover up their blunders. For example, Heinrich Böhm (Chief Torpedo Mechanic of U377) was checking the torpedo tubes and pressed the firing button before switching it off. The lost torpedo was accounted for by later firing two and recording a salvo of three. Other errors, made in the heat of battle, perhaps involving diving controls or guns, could have had more serious consequences. Many of the mistakes made by commanders which have been recorded in the U-boat Command's diary were of the most elementary nature. For example, in June 1941 KL Rolf Mützelburg (U203) attacked when he should have waited for other boats to join him. He then withdrew in order to repair some minor damage and Dönitz used the radio to order him back to the convoy, saying that repairs could wait until other boats arrived to take over the shadowing task. U66 (KL Richard Zapp) returned home because he thought (mistakenly) that the maximum diving depth with external torpedo doors jammed open was 50 metres. KL Heinrich Driver (U371) travelled too fast to his operations area,

One of the Atlantic boats of Type VIIC at sea with distinctive saddle tanks clearly visible. The narrow, long commander's pennant can be seen flying from the commander's flag pole. The photo, looking forward from aft of the conning tower, shows the deck bulge around the big gun.

consumed too much fuel and ran short shortly before a convoy was due to run into his sights. KL Wolf Stiebler (U61) drove his machinery too hard, causing several avoidable faults, and tactical errors prevented him from attacking. And so the story goes on. These incidents, all listed in Dönitz's diary, do suggest that a more comprehensive training might have produced better results. At the same time, it should be emphasised that none of these men were beginners; all of them had considerable experience and, indeed, Mützelburg and Zapp were holders of the Knights Cross of the Iron Cross.

Once boats had left the Baltic, there appears to have been little or no organised operational training. To make matters worse, instructors often thought that graduating boats were of poor standard, but only about two boats out of a dozen from each course could be failed. The rest had to be pushed out to the front whether they stood a chance against the enemy or not. The nature of the training is also most interesting. Very little has been written about the training programmes in the Baltic but at times it would appear as if they bore little relation to the conditions which would be experienced at the front. It has been claimed that instructors were kept up-to-date with the latest developments, but there does not seem to be much evidence of this. In 1945, for example, Type VIIC boats were still learning the intricacies of convoy attack, although it had been impossible to get anywhere near convoys for 18 months and the bitter fighting during the autumn of 1943 should have finally proved that such old, conventional boats could not match the escorts' opposition. Another most interesting aspect of the education process was the lack of emphasis on reality in operational training, and as Dönitz said, 'The intricacies have to be learned by facing the enemy'. To give an example, towards the end of the war U-boats practised raising and lowering the schnorkel and cruising with it for relatively short periods. Once technically proficient, the men went into the Atlantic and soon experienced the difficulties of carrying out the procedure in rough waters for long periods while at the same time being harried by the allied escorts. In Britain, the Royal Navy tackled the problem very differently and made every effort to simulate combat conditions.

Of almost equal significance to personnel and training were the ships themselves. Germany began the Atlantic offensive mainly with medium Type VII and long-range Type IX U-boats. The first have been described by Dönitz as being ideally suited for their task and both have been proclaimed as excellent craft. But the fact is that

Probably U229 (OL Robert Schetelig) supplying fuel to U377 (Otto Köhler) on 27 May 1943. The conning tower configuration is of interest. The Type 1 anti-aircraft gun platform modification has been fitted with two single 20mm weapons, but the 88mm quick-firing gun is still in place. Also note that there are two jumping wires at the front. This was necessary because the radar aerial only worked straight ahead and transmitted its signals between the two wires.

these U-boats, produced between the two wars, were not much different, other than in minor modifications, from the vessels of World War I. Furthermore, they lacked the potential for any drastic modifications. The 1920s saw a revolution in the German ship-building industry resulting in the construction of three pocket battleships which incorporated a number of highly revolutionary features which made them the envy of the rest of the world. Unfortunately, it appears that none of the innovative thought used to beat the terms of the Versailles Treaty permeated through to the submarine industry. Instead, naval architects and the Supreme Naval Command were content to accept modified revisions of old designs. The electro U-boats of Types XXI and XXIII, which were built towards the end of the war and heralded as a revolution in submarine history, contained virtually no technology which had not been available during the 1930s when the foundation stone for the U-boat Arm of World War II was being laid. Type XXI was made more efficient by installing semi-automatic, hydraulic torpedo loading gear which could re-load six tubes in less time than it took to do one tube in a VIIC. The boats were made to go faster by adding more batteries; there were built-in ventilation systems and better food storage facilities, and the toilets could be used in depths deeper than 25 metres. They contained no revolutionary innovations which were not technically feasible during the 1930s. It appears as if Germany was content with the boat as developed during World War I and did not feel it necessary to plan or design boats for the future. This was not done until Dönitz had the opportunity of influencing construction and by then it was much too late.

In Britain, the situation was different. The few destroyers in service at the beginning of the war were designed to support heavy ships in coastal waters and they lacked the endurance to sail long distances with convoys. Deep sea trawlers were first adapted to meet the demand of protecting convoys while a new anti-submarine vessel, the corvette, was developed from a trawler design. Although the type which evolved was slow and could not overtake surfaced U-boats, it was ideally suited to the rigours of convoy-defence and became the backbone of the anti-submarine fleets. Other ships, such as frigates and escort carriers, were later introduced whose main purpose was to force U-boats under and then depth charge them. Aircraft also played a major role, and began to make a serious impact from the autumn of 1942. Following an early skirmish with the escort carrier *Audacity*, Dönitz said, 'The chances of being sunk are greater than the prospects of success'. But though he recognised the danger from the air, he did not fully appreciate the real threat that it posed. Even as late as the summer of 1943, he was still of the opinion that the battle against aircraft could be won. Unfortunately for the Germans, the planned anti-aircraft weapons either failed or could not be produced in time.

A further difference between the two countries can be seen when evaluating their weapons. Initially, each U-boat was fitted with torpedo tubes, a 20mm anti-aircraft gun, a large quick-firing gun of either 88mm or 105mm calibre and a few small machine guns. The larger boats often carried a 37mm quick-firing gun as well. KL Herbert Schultze (U48) has drawn attention to some of the problems associated with this artillery when he said: 'On the two occasions when we tried the 88mm gun, it was only our lucky angel who left me with the gun crew still on board. Injuries and the danger of being washed overboard did not make it worthwhile'. Opportunities for using the heavy guns diminished after 1940 while the need for anti-aircraft armament increased. The two most common Atlantic U-boats, Types VII and IX, could not be adapted to carry sufficient fire power for shooting down fast-flying armoured planes before these had the opportunity of dropping their depth charges. Anti-

Officers relaxing at Lagona near Brest. Second from the left is OL Gerhard Kluth, who was killed by his own acoustic torpedo in U377. The boat's engineering officer, OL Karl-Heinz Nitschke, on his left, was transferred before the last fateful voyage.

aircraft guns on U-boats remained unsatisfactory all through the war, and could only be used as mild deterrents unless favourable conditions allowed a few lucky hits in vital parts to bring an adversary down.

The German problems with torpedoes, which came to a head during the Norwegian Campaign of 1940, is well known today. The causes were not fully understood during the war because three faults, mentioned earlier, contributed to the problem and this combination was not identified at the time. Torpedo failures plagued U-boats until the very end of the conflict. At one stage during the war British propaganda departments wanted to expose the success rate claimed by the Germans but the Admiralty recognised that the exaggerated claims of the U-boat crews hid some of the real problems associated with the torpedoes. One example of Germany's over-estimation involved the acoustic torpedoes of Type Zaunkönig (T5) which was calculated by the U-boat Command as having had a 50 percent success rate, but after the war it was learned that only 77 ships were sunk using over 700 torpedoes, which made the real success rate around 11 percent.

On the allied side, the situation was a very different one. At the beginning of the war the Royal Navy and the Royal Air Force were issued with quite ineffective weapons which were, however, improved significantly as the war continued. For example, to begin

The First Officer of the Dutch freighter Maddera *(van der Tuurs) on the bows of U591 (KL Hansjürgen Zetsche) about to be taken aboard the homeward-bound U758 (KL Helmut Manseck). The* Maddera *had been sunk on 24 February 1943 by U653 (KL Gerhard Feiler), which suggests that U591 found van der Tuurs adrift.*

with the depth settings on depth charges were too deep, and thus gave U-boats enough time to move out of the way before they exploded. This was rectified and the charges were also filled with a better explosive. Then came the Hedgehog, an ahead throwing mortar. The Royal Air Force began the war with anti-submarine bombs which were supposed to detonate on impact, but the first two also brought down the planes which had dropped them. Then came aerial depth charges, which were also improved as time progressed.

The balance of the Battle of the Atlantic was held not with explosives, but by mastering new fields of technology. Radar made it possible to see in the dark, while the Leigh Light was developed to aid aircraft spot U-boats once they were too close for radar contact. HF/DF pin-pointed the sources of radio transmissions and helped ships determine the likely directions of impending attacks. Britain was initially plagued by equipment being unable to withstand seawater, but this was also rectified.

By the beginning of 1943 convoy defences were able to withstand U-boat attacks principally because of information from Special Intelligence (ie the ability to understand the German radio code) which made it possible to either route convoys away from wolf packs or direct warships and aircraft towards them. If U-boats did manage to reach convoys, their usual broadcast at the start of an attack warned escorts of the imminent danger and the number of transmissions told them how many to expect. Meanwhile, HF/DF indicated the direction from which they would be coming. Radar-equipped ships were then deployed to seek out the attacker and, once he was forced under, Asdic helped to place explosives in the most effective spot.

A large part of the allied success was due to scientists working with the armed forces. They visited operations rooms and ships at sea in order to understand the problems faced by the men at the front. For example, Professor P M S Blackett (Chief of Operational Research at Admiralty) was reputed to have visited the operations room of the Western Approaches in Liverpool and concluded that Coastal Command was having difficulty spotting U-boats because their conspicuous black aircraft were easily spotted and this allowed the U-boats plenty of time to dive. After he suggested that the aircraft were painted white it became more difficult for U-boat lookouts to spot them and the number of sightings increased dramatically. In Germany this only started to happen in a most limited way during 1943, and by that time it was too late. Scientists could only provide the barest means for avoiding the full weight of the allied onslaught.

Not only operational research, but also intelligence was given a high priority on the allied side. By 1944, men in the secret sub-marine tracking room at the Admiralty in London knew more about U-boat operations than the majority of German submarine and flotilla commanders. The Royal Navy knew how wolf packs worked; how individuals attacked; how deep U-boats could dive; how fast they could cruise; how often German lookouts cleaned their binoculars; when they were at the end of their watches and likely to be tired and so on. This information was published on a monthly basis in magazine form and made it possible for men at the front to learn the habits of their adversaries. On the German side virtually nothing was known about the British or Americans. U-boats usually went to sea with scanty, out-of-date information and latest details were broadcast while they were on their way to their operations areas.

In 1941, Britain started to introduce a few minor, but effective countermeasures and from then on, Germany was always a few steps behind, trying to find ways of neutralising the latest allied advances. Therefore, the turning point of the U-boat offensive came long before 1943. May 1943 was simply the first month when all these factors came together with dramatic effect.

The German naval ensign at sea.

19. Leuthen – In the Steps of Frederick the Great

Though May 1943 is regarded by most commentators as marking the end of the U-boat offensive, German leaders saw the situation at the time rather differently. The rank and file, who were unaware of latest weapon developments and purposely kept in the dark in order to prevent any breach of security, saw little point in going on, but senior officers were more optimistic. They were not expecting Germany to win the war, but they hoped to be able to hold on long enough for the secret weapons, already under construction, to help them negotiate a peace. This optimism was due largely to poor intelligence, which gave them a false idea of allied developments. For example, contrary to German knowledge, since the end of 1942, the allied ship construction industry was producing more ships than were being sunk.

The summer of 1943 saw the culmination of several German projects, which Dönitz thought would provide the tools for reversing the recent downward trend in the Atlantic.

First, conning tower modifications to accommodate more guns, which had been in progress since the end of 1942, had not yet made the anticipated impact because the armament was still missing. So far, boats had been equipped with a variety of double or single 20mm weapons, supplemented with small calibre machine guns. The first of the new 20mm quadruple AA guns appeared in the French bases during May 1943 and over 50 of them had been fitted by the end of July. The automatic 37mm anti-aircraft gun, which differed considerably from the earlier quick-firing gun of the same calibre, was due to be delivered to the front for the autumn. These weapons were designed to fire a new type of high explosive shell, known as a mine shell, whose projectiles were three times the weight of the earlier ammunition.

Second, the U-boat Command placed high hopes on the new radar detector which was due to come to the front in August. Known as Wanze (from Hagenuk–Wellenanzeiger), it had the great advantage of searching automatically through radar wavebands. It was capable of picking up a wider range of radar frequencies than existing Metox or Grandin equipment, could cope with intermittent radar transmissions and did not radiate conspicuous signals. This last characteristic was, in fact, irrelevant, but during the

U377 (OL Gerhard Kluth) running into Brest with damage sustained during a series of bitter attacks against convoys while participating as a member of Group LEUTHEN, Dönitz's first major strike in the North Atlantic after the disastrous losses of May 1943. The two rings by the side of the hole are the tops of retractable bollards.

summer of 1943, when German scientists had still failed to discover how U-boats were being detected, they feared signals emitted by Metox and Grandin radar detectors were the cause. Since March 1943, the use of short wave radar which could not be detected by Wanze put Britain one step ahead again. Similar apparatus to this ASV (air to surface vessel) Mark III had been captured in a bomber brought down near Rotterdam in Holland. German experts, responsible for its reconstruction, declared it suitable for finding large industrial targets, but they did not believe it capable of picking up objects as small as submarines.

Two other innovations were radar foxers and anti-destroyer torpedoes. Two types of decoy were becoming available. Aphrodite consisted of a hydrogen filled balloon, supporting bands of metal foil which simulated a surfaced U-boat, while Thetis, used mainly in the Bay of Biscay, was a simple three-dimensional cross with foil strung between the struts. The first anti-escort torpedoes of Type

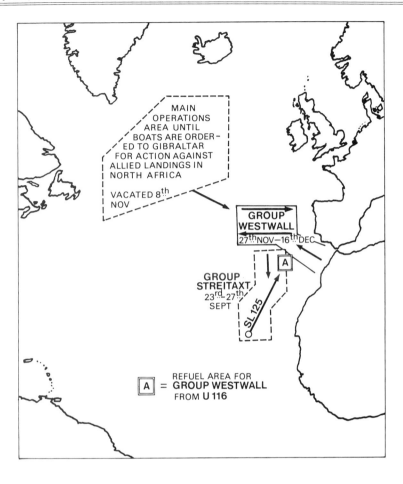

U-boat operations: end of 1942.

Group STREITAXT, set up on 24 October 1942

U134	KL	Rudolf Schendel
U203	KL	Hermann Kottmann
U409	OL	Hanns-Ferdinand Massmann
U509	KL	Werner Witte
U510	FK	Karl Neitzel
U572	KL	Heinz Hirsacker
U604	KL	Horst Höltring
U659	KL	Hans Stock

Group WESTWALL, established during the end of November 1942.

U86	KL	Walter Schug
U91	KL	Heinz Walkerling
U92	KL	Adolf Oelrich
U98	OL	Kurt Eichmann
U155	KK	Adolf Piening
U185	KL	August Maus
U218	KL	Richard Becker
U263	KL	Kurt Nölke
U411	KL	Johann Spindlegger
U413	KL	Gustav Poel
U515	KL	Werner Henke
U519	KL	Günter Eppen
U564	OL	Hans Fiedler
U566	OL	Gerhard Remus
U613	KL	Helmut Köppe
U653	KL	Gerhard Feiler

Falke had been introduced in March 1943 when U603 (OL Hans-Joachim Bertelsmann), U758 (KL Helmuth Manseck) and U221 (KL Hans Trojer) used them against convoys HX229 and SC122. The improved version, Type Zaunkönig or T5, was faster, had a greater range and could be used with either magnetic or contact detonators. It was thought capable of sinking small attacking craft and able to prevent situations like an incident in May when one escort had simultaneously forced six U-boats away because none of them had weapons for fighting back. It might be interesting to add that the findings of a detailed analysis of the anti-convoy torpedo (known as FAT) became available in May, but the data provided a false picture because U-boats were frequently forced under and could not observe the results. Hearing a detonation, they assumed their target had sunk. As a result, the zig-zagging and loop running torpedo was estimated as having had a success rate as high as 75 percent and this made a significant contribution to the U-boat Command's optimism.

∗   ∗   ∗

After the heavy losses in May, Dönitz ordered an evacuation out of the dangerous waters. Boats low on fuel were ordered home while others were told not to take any risks and then directed into southern waters away from enemy aircraft. Eight were sent into the Western Approaches to send signals simulating the assembly of a wolf pack. Dönitz considered it important to maintain a presence at sea, to keep up-to-date with latest enemy procedures and to be ready for the next convoy attack with the new weapons. Going further afield was facilitated by the availability in May of several new supply U-boats of Type XIV. U460 (KL Ebe Schnoor) had been near the Cape Verde Islands since the beginning of the month. U463 (KK Leo Wolfbauer), U488 (OL Erwin Bartke) and a mine-layer of Type XB, U118 (KK Werner Czygan), were ready to leave in May and two more supply boats, U462 (OL Bruno Vowe) and U487 (OL Helmut Metz) followed at the end of the month.

Apart from boats diverted from the North Atlantic, 11 long-range boats of Group MONSOON were on their way to the Far East. The first had left in March and sailings continued until summer. None of these managed to avoid the onslaught of the enemy and Group MONSOON lost three boats before reaching the South Atlantic.

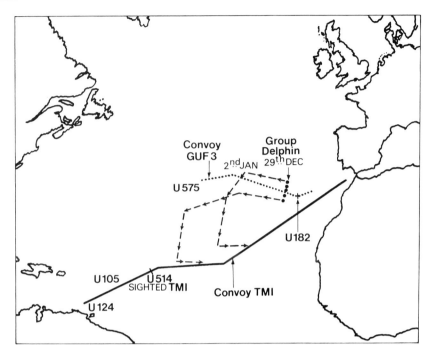

*Convoy TM1. December 1942
to January 1943.*

Group DELPHIN

U514	KL	Hans-Jürgen Auffermann
U381	KL	Wilhelm Heinrich, Graf von Pückler und Limpurg
U571	KL	Helmuth Möhlmann
U442	KL	Hans-Jürgen Hesse
U620	KL	Heinz Stein
U575	KL	Günther Heydemann
U436	KL	Günther Seibicke
U125	KL	Ulrich Folkers

Two outward bound boats

U511	KL	Fritz Schneewind
U522	KL	Herbert Schneider

and two homeward bound boats

U181	KK	Wolfgang Luth
U134	KL	Rudolf Schendel

were also directed towards the tankers

British aircraft patrolling the Black Pit of Biscay had become the biggest problem. The story of the first aircraft trap, U441 (KL Götz von Hartmann; KL Klaus Hartmann commanded the boat before and after him) which started operations during the summer of 1943 is well known today. Ten such conversions, each carrying a quadruple 20mm, a single 37mm and two twin 20mm AA guns, were ordered shortly before U441 went into the action which killed ten and wounded thirteen. The boat's medical officer patched up the injured and then brought the boat home because commander and officers had been incapacitated. None of these aircraft traps was successful and they were converted back into their original configurations before the end of the year. To overcome the increased fire power of the aircraft traps, the Royal Air Force introduced the new tactic of launching simultaneous attacks from different directions. To combat this, U-boats were ordered to cross the Bay in small groups, but even the combined fire power of five or more

U262 with anti-aircraft armament on display. On the left is a 37mm, on the upper platform two 20mm twins and on the conning tower wall a light machine gun. The bulge on the side of the conning tower, where the jumping wires are attached, housed additional radar equipment, armour and a metal cupboard-like structure as defence against aircraft.

boats had little effect. Two boats of the first group, U68 (OL Albert Lauzemis) and U155 (KK Adolf Piening), were hit hard enough to be forced back to port. Damaged boats and injured men were becoming a new problem and the difficulties are well illustrated by the attack on U564 (OL Hans Fiedler) in mid June 1943. The attacking aircraft was shot down, but not before inflicting heavy damage. U185 (KL August Maus) was diverted to escort the stricken boat back home, but the two had only just joined forces when another aircraft sank U564.

The U-boat Command reacted by suggesting new routes through the Bay of Biscay. In future boats were to travel south along the French coast and, to break out in a westerly direction closer to Spain where land-based aircraft from England, at their extreme range, could only operate for a short time. Unfortunately for the Germans, Britain had taken advantage of the evacuation of the North Atlantic and sent hunter-killer groups to plug the weak spot. Two U-boats, U119 (KL Horst-Tessen von Kameke) and U449 (OL Hermann Otto) were sunk by such blockading forces during June, and Dönitz began to think that there was the very real possibility of the enemy shutting down the French bases. Boats were told to run only on electric motors when crossing the danger area to make it easier for lookouts to hear approaching aircraft. But it did not work. The noises made by water washing through the vents in the side of the hull were too loud and the charging of batteries became too much of a problem. U383 (KL Horst Kremser) was travelling on electric motors when it was damaged a few hundred miles out from Brest. U218 (KL Richard Becker), U454 (KL Burghard Hackländer), U706 (KL Alexander von Zitzewitz) and three torpedo boats were instructed to help. Two of the U-boats were damaged during the approach and U383 was sunk before the remaining rescuers could reach it. The torpedo boats were then diverted to assist U106 (OL Wolf-Dietrich Damerau), which had also been damaged in an air attack. Waiting down below, Damerau only surfaced when the distinctive high pitched wine of the MTBs could be heard on the hydrophones. Aerial depth charges damaged the boat shortly after it had surfaced and only a few survivors remained for the torpedo boats. The Bay of Biscay was becoming a no-go area.

August 1943 saw events turn a little for the better. For weeks, Dönitz had been telling U-boat men that new weapons would soon bring improvements and he was just beginning to doubt his own propaganda when fortunes suddenly changed. Shortly after telling the Supreme Naval Command in confidence, 'U-boat operations in

U172 (*Carl Emmermann*) *with an early form of radar on the conning tower and the members of the gun crew with harness belts.*

U172 (Carl Emmermann) with fixed radar on the top of the conning tower. The signals from this gear went straight ahead so that the boat had to sail in a circle for a 360-degree sweep. The boat is a Type IXC with 105mm gun.

the South Atlantic have not achieved the anticipated results and the Bay of Biscay is becoming considerably more dangerous', 80 acoustic torpedoes of Type Zaunkönig arrived ahead of schedule. At the same time, the Hagenuk radar detector (known as Wanze) was achieving successes. In mid September, Dönitz told his men, 'the radar war has changed in our favour'.

Commanders were receiving limited instruction in using acoustic torpedoes and the Hagenuk radar detectors, while Dönitz planned to amass enough boats to renew convoy attacks in the North Atlantic. He named the Group LEUTHEN after a village in Silesia where the King of Prussia, Frederick the Great, had defeated the Austrians against overwhelming odds. U460 (KL Friedrich Schäfer), a supply boat of Type XIV, was positioned some 200 miles east of Newfoundland with a view of refuelling those who had been out for some time and the rest of the pack was made up of fresh boats from France. They were equipped with Hagenuk radar detectors, acoustic torpedoes of Type Zaunkönig, the new anti-convoy FAT torpedoes and heavier anti-aircraft armament. It was intended to move the group secretly into the convoy routes and then to work with small numbers in approaching as close as possible to the merchant ships. This was difficult to coordinate as boats had to maintain radio silence and had no means of communicating with each other, except by using signal lamps. The radar detector was intended to prevent surprise attacks and the orders were to dive as soon as aircraft or surface ships came into sight. After sufficient boats had gathered around the target, the signal 'Remain on the surface' was to mark the start of an attack and each boat would then run in, guns ready to deal with aircraft and acoustic torpedoes to sink escorts. To make matters more difficult for the enemy, and in case the radio code had been compromised, positions were given in a further code so that only U-boat commanders and the operations room on land knew their exact meaning.

The plan went well. There were hardly any problems in reaching the assembly area in the air gap of the mid-Atlantic. The German radio monitoring service (B-Dienst under Heinz Bonatz) identified only one boat, U341 (OL Dietrich Epp), as having been spotted by enemy aircraft while moving north into the patrol line. The plan had been to gather the boats a considerable distance south and only order them into a searching formation at the last moment before the convoy was expected. U341 was sunk by Squadron 10 of the Royal Canadian Airforce on the assembly day, 19 September. The other U-boats were in luck in that the fast convoy ON202, which had sailed from Liverpool on 15 September, was catching up the slower convoy ONS18 and at 1200 hours on 20 September the two were ordered to join forces and, for some time, about 50 merchant ships were scattered over a large area, while two escort groups had to form up into one. The warships had been warned of the wolf pack and the HF/DF had been indicating transmissions around the convoy since the afternoon of the nineteenth. Luckily for the merchentmen, the U-boats had lost contact and were unaware of the merger. When the simultaneous attack was ordered by KL Manfred Kinzel (U338), with the signal 'Remain on the surface', there were too few boats in position to create any serious problems for the enemy and it was possible for escorts to focus on those running in. This was the first convoy attack with the new Zaunkönig acoustic torpedo, and it also happened that U338 was one of the first U-boats to be sunk by an acoustic homing torpedo, of Type Fido. This was dropped from an aircraft of RAF Squadron 120 shortly after Kinzel had started his run in on 20 September.

During the first attacks, 15 acoustic torpedoes were fired against escorts. Seven ships were recorded as definitely sunk and three more as probable. The other five missed, possibly because commanders shot from too great a range. Despite their losses, the inner ring of convoy defences was not broken, but the Germans were nonetheless pleased with the results. It was felt that during the following night the U-boats should be brought within striking distance of the merchant ships. Throughout the twenty-first they kept in contact by using radar detectors and hydrophones. Things seemed to be going well until thick fog engulfed the scene shortly before the attack was due to start. Although contact was maintained, it was impossible to go in. The effectiveness of the British radar was clearly demonstrated by the way in which escorts pursued U-boats through thick fog. U377 (OL Gerhard Kluth) only just managed to dive before a collision. On returning to the surface during the afternoon of the twenty-second, the men of U377 found conditions improving, but the occasional ray of sun through the shifting mist brought air support and it was not long before the boat was engaged in a gun duel. Flight Lieutenant J R Martin, from Gander in Newfoundland, was put off his aim by U377's impressive fire power, but his own guns inflicted considerable damage and a number of men, including Kluth and the navigator of the aircraft, were seriously injured. Kluth was brought below while Martin circled out of gun range, calling for support. Ernst-August Gerke (IWO) took command while the wounded were lowered into the boat.

1 November 1944, on board U318 (OL Josef Will). Earlier in the war, U-boat men were issued only with head protection against the natural elements, but once aircraft started to make their presence felt, tin hats became vital items for gun crews.

The battle was abandoned a day later. By then, U-boats had been in action for four days and even crews which had not suffered any serious casualties were worn out. The U-boat Command was under the impression that 12 escorts had been sunk while another three were classed as 'probable sinkings' and a good number of merchant ships were also thought to have gone down. The new anti-aircraft guns were considered to have been a great success, but it was not realised that very few aircraft had been employed against Group LEUTHEN, poor visibility along the coasts having grounded the majority of them. On account of these successes, KA Eberhard Godt (chief of the U-boat Command) sent a signal congratulating the men for their efforts.

The true figures were not so impressive. Six merchant ships and three escorts sunk and one escort was damaged. On the other side, three U-boats were sunk and another three seriously damaged.

The German acoustic torpedo had an arming range of 400 metres, this being the distance a torpedo had to travel before the detonators could activate the explosive. The idea was to prevent an accidental explosion until it was far enough away not to damage, or even destroy, the boat which fired it. However, with a sound detection head homing in on the loudest noise in the vicinity, there was a possibility of the torpedo turning round and aiming itself at the U-boat which fired it. To prevent such accidents, U-boat commanders were ordered to dive to 60 metres after having fired a T5 from a bow tube while a stern shot was to be followed by extreme silence. In practice, this did not work out. Men thought this depth to be too near the surface to withstand depth charges and the majority went considerably deeper. As a result they were not able to observe the target at the moment of impact and the confusing noises which the hydrophones received made it impossible to determine exactly what had happened. During the autumn of 1943 the sinking figures reported by commanders were accepted almost without question and it was not until early 1944 that doubts began to creep in. Although the U-boat Command later realised that there was a discrepancy between actual sinkings and figures quoted by U-boat commanders, the poor results were not fully comprehended at the time.

Both the FAT and T5 torpedoes suffered from detonator problems which were a hangover from the torpedo crisis at the beginning of the war. The fault was demonstrated during the first attack by the LEUTHEN Group when HMS *Lagan*'s propellers were blown off by U270 (KL Paul-Friedrich Otto). The torpedo should have exploded under the hull but instead detonated some distance behind the ship. In the majority of cases the detonations occurred even further away. This was later put down to the foxer, towed by escorts to attract the acoustic torpedoes, or 'gnats' as they were known in the Royal Navy. Decoys should have made no difference to the functioning of the T5 because it was designed to cope with any number of distractions, whether towed or in an ejected buoy, and detonate under the target if the magnetic pistol was switched on, or on hitting the side of the hull if percussion was to be used. Problems with magnetic detonators made them unusable in rough seas while the design of the percussion prongs was such that the head of the torpedo tended to bounce off the shallow rounded warship hull without exploding.

These defeats were not fully appreciated by the U-boat Command at the time and September ended on a fairly optimistic note with successes anticipated in the following months.

20. The Disasters Continue with Rossbach

October 1943 to January 1944

The high hopes which were placed on Group LEUTHEN, the first group armed with improved anti-aircraft armament and the acoustic torpedoes of Type Zaunkönig, were soon dispelled by a number of serious setbacks. These involved Group ROSSBACH which was deployed to intercept 21 ships of convoy ON 203. The German Radio Monitoring Service had discovered the route in good time, but on the 27 September the convoy avoided the patrol line by diverting to the north. At about the same time, convoy ONS 203 used similar tactics to evade ROSSBACH and, while the U-boat Command was digesting the bad news, convoy HX 258 skirted around the southern end of the formation. This was hard to swallow especially as the convoys had been detected in good time. To make matters worse, the Allies continued not only to locate U-boats during the darkest of nights but also to pursue them with accuracy and severity. The German tactics of remaining on the surface to fight aircraft with the improved AA armament failed miserably. Seven of the 21 ROSSBACH boats were lost as a result of sudden air attacks. Back at U-boat Command, an analysis attributed the failure of this group to an unfortunate combination of circumstances such as bad weather, poor visibility, mechanical breakdowns and boats being forced under at critical moments and plans went ahead for another offensive.

Knowing that it would be futile to attempt the next attack in the same area, boats with enough fuel were ordered south to become the core of a new group named SCHLIEFFEN. The targeted convoy, ON 206 with 65 ships, was detected by the Radio Monitoring Service and first sighted on 15 October by U844 (OL Günther Möller). While converging on the convoy, another boat, U964 (OL Emmo Hummerjohann), ran into the 52 ships of ONS 20 and experienced the same ferocious defence as had the boats of Group ROSSBACH. Only two U-boats, U426 (KL Christian Reich) and U309 (Hans-Gert Mahrholz), managed to get close enough to shoot at merchant ships. During the late hours of 15 October, U426 sank the 6000 GRT freighter *Essex Lance* straggling behind ONS 20 and two days later U309 fired a salvo of four FAT torpedoes into the convoy. Two FAT explosions were heard after a running time of almost 15 minutes, but there are no reports of ships having been

U181 (KK Kurt Freiwald) showing the 37mm anti-aircraft gun on the lower, rear platform. This photograph was taken in the approaches to Penang, where U181 was surrounded by a variety of interesting local craft.

attacked and it is assumed that they had detonated at the ends of their runs. In return for these successes, the dozen or so boats in the SCHLIEFFEN group received a devastating battering, resulting in the loss of six of them in two days. The term success is used deliberately in the plural because a penetration of convoy defences was already considered to be a great achievement. The U-boat Command had to make drastic alterations in its strategy to avoid the entire fleet being sacrificed. Despite the allied successes, there was no time to celebrate in Whitehall. The Naval Intelligence's correct forecast of an increasing number of boats due to appear at the front kept pressure at maximum.

Shortly after the bitter defeat of Groups ROSSBACH and SCHLIEF-FEN, boats from LEUTHEN returned home and made a detailed analysis of the situation possible. This showed that there had been a considerable increase in the number of aircraft around convoys, even though for most of the time the Canadian Air Force had been grounded by fog. Furthermore, it appeared as if the enemy had developed a distinctly new approach to fighting U-boats. Previously, the Bay of Biscay had been the major blackspot for sudden aircraft attack, but now it seemed that the majority of U-boats managed to pass through the area without serious incident. Most of the attacks by aircraft were taking place in the operations areas. The appearance of the new anti-aircraft guns had brought a brief respite while the opposition sized up the impressive display of tracer shells. Once it was realised there was more bark than bite the attacks became more determined than ever and the 20mm quadruple proved a poor defence. The armoured long-range aircraft could soak up over a hundred hits and still deliver their attacks with deadly accuracy, though in a few skirmishes aircraft were brought down after they had dropped depth charges. The first new 20mm quadruples were hasty conversions of army guns and the U-boat Command thought there was no point in improving the design. The guns were too weak and too difficult to operate. The 20mm twin, which had also been installed from June onwards, was considered to be a better weapon. Technically it was far superior as it was able to resist seawater better and firing it from shoulder supports was much easier than controlling the quadruple's hand wheels. The problem of insufficient space on the already enlarged platform was overcome by adding another few centimetres of floor space. The original idea of eliminating obstructions by leaving off gun shields was acknowledged to have been a mistake and orders were given to provide protection for the upper gun crews. The trials with three 37mm automatic anti-aircraft guns had been a great success and by the end of 1943 over 20 were being used in the Atlantic. These weapons differed from earlier 37mm quick-firing guns, which had their shells inserted singly into the muzzle and they had the advantage over the smaller calibre by having a greater hitting power as well as an almost 1000-metre-long tracer path.

The first stopgap measure, taken as a result of the ROSSBACH losses, was to modify the wolf pack technique by using smaller patrol lines and not assembling the boats until the last possible moment so making it more difficult for the Allies to determine their positions. Orders were given to remain submerged during the day and, when surfaced at night, to dive as soon as the radar detector produced a response. This tactic meant that it took two to three weeks to travel as far west as Cape Farewell (the southern tip of Greenland) and the requirement for fast travel during the hours of

U703, a Type VIIC, probably photographed during the late spring of 1943, shortly before OL Joachim Brünner took over command from KL Heinz Bielfeld. The barrels, with holes, of three light machine guns are visible. A partly extended rod aerial can be seen on the left. Machine guns had already been issued to U-boats during the first months of the war, but were hardly used. A new function was found for them in 1943, when they were reissued as an interim measure to help fend off aircraft.

darkness led to heavy fuel consumption. The primary objective now was simply to remain at sea. Sinkings became regarded as a secondary objective and the men going to sea were told that 'it is important for you to remain at sea to keep enemy forces occupied and to prevent the ships and aircraft from being employed against your families at home'.

Although the disastrous results led many senior officers to conclude that U-boats were no longer capable of tackling convoys, there were, nevertheless, three good reasons for continuing with the campaign. First, a number of long-range aircraft of Type Junker 290 were made available for reconnaissance. Second, the successes with the acoustic torpedoes were believed to have been considerable, eliminating a good number of escorts. Third, the availability of the new 37mm anti-aircraft gun, which was expected to be able to bring down allied planes before they got close enough to damage U-boats, would make it possible to operate in the eastern Atlantic, closer to the British Isles.

Early in November, mid-North Atlantic operations were abandoned and new attempts made to concentrate in the area to the west of Spain. In December, there followed a thrust into the approaches of the North Channel (the waters between Ireland and Scotland), which Günter Hessler and Albert Hoschatt described as a 'withdrawal to the eastern Atlantic'. Neither of these moves did much to relieve the general situation. Sighting reports from long-range aircraft frequently arrived in the operations room after reports from the Radio Monitoring Service containing details of decrypted British signals about the very same aircraft. U515 (KL Werner Henke) was lucky enough to lie in the path of a convoy, but was forced under before ships came into sight and before a report could be transmitted. U515's luck lay in the fact that the convoy passed almost overhead and the propeller disturbance made it impossible for Asdics to get a bearing on the U-boat. Yet the hunters did not give up and kept U515 down for ten hours, long enough for the convoy to travel safely past. Such attacks led the U-boat Command to conclude that 'the second and especially the third night of an attack is becoming impossible. The enemy is capable of accurately locating U-boats at night and engages them effectively with aircraft or strong surface forces. In future, operations must be planned for one night only'.

The number of German aircraft flying each day had not increased appreciably since the first attempts at co-operation with the Luftwaffe and, once again, this demonstrated the difficulties of carrying out proper reconnaissance with only a few planes. Konteradmiral Eberhard Godt (chief of the U-boat Command) noted it was pointless for convoy positions to be established only once or even twice a day. Details of positions were needed at least every four hours, otherwise it was impossible to direct U-boats into position ahead of the merchant ships. Mechanical defects in the aircraft added to the frustration. Towards the end of 1943, the U-boat Reconnaissance Squadron consisted of 17 Ju 290s, two Ju 88s, three FW 200s and two BV 222s. Five aircraft suffered from engine trouble, two had radar or radio defects and three were out of action due to unspecified faults. The lack of proper maintenance, due mainly to the high proportion of time the planes were kept airborne, was partly responsible. But even with all of them in the air, there were too few and Godt emphasised the need for more. His criticism that air crews had not enough training for their reconnaissance duties brought an immediate rebuttal from the Luftwaffe which produced evidence to show that convoys had been trailed correctly and that the fault for not sinking ships lay with the poor calibre of the U-boat commanders. Whilst the Allies inevitably suffered con-

Opposite: The anti-aircraft armament of U952 (KL Oskar Curio). Two 20mm twins are visible near the camera and a 20mm quadruple on the lower platform. The first-mentioned proved to have been quite good for U-boats because shooting them from the shoulder made it relatively easy to track fast flying planes. The shoulder supports of the starboard gun are visible to the left of the man's face, just aft of the grid over the ventilation shaft. The quadruple had to be moved by handwheels, making it somewhat difficult to train on fast-moving targets from an unstable base.

OL Gerhard Matschulat
commissioning U247 on 23
October 1943 with a 20mm
quadruple anti-aircraft gun
clearly visible. The dome at
Matschulat's feet is the lid to a
pressure-resistant ammunition
container, and the open galley
hatch can be seen in the
foreground. Note the
navigation light on the rail.

Towards the end of the war
schnorkels were vital for
survival. This photo, taken in
drydock in Penang, shows an
improvised breathing pipe
being fitted to U181 before the
planned return to Europe.
Mechanical failure later
prevented this voyage.

Maat Kirchner of U251 with a machine gun attached to the conning tower wall. The device above his head is a radar detection aerial and note the signal lamp clipped to the periscope support. Kirchner is wearing an uninflated life jacket.

Bootsmaat Willi Pohle, who was usually responsible for shooting the gun, with OL Teddy Suhren making a delicate adjustment to the 20mm deck gun.

siderable interforce rivalry, co-operation between different units was constantly improved through the war and this played a significant role in their success. In Germany, Godt's criticism appears to have created nothing but charges and counter charges, but no constructive discussion which might have improved the situation.

The latest anti-aircraft armament, made up of the new 37mm gun and used off Spain and in the approaches to the North Channel, did not live up to expectations. The additional weight, which made the boats top heavy and caused them to roll 30 degrees and sometimes even 60 degrees, put considerable strain on the crews, reduced the lookouts' vision and, worst of all, neutralised the increased range of the bigger gun because it was too difficult to aim. The longer tracer path of almost a kilometre clearly showed the shells flying wide of their mark and emphasised the difficulty of shooting from such unstable platforms.

Following the U-boats' experiences off North Channel in December 1943, operational orders were amended as follows. During daylight, boats were to remain submerged between periscope depth and 25 metres where they could still receive long-wave radio transmissions without extending an aerial above the surface of the water. If a convoy was located the commander was to attack at once and report the details later. Contrary to earlier orders, he was to break away as soon as strong enemy forces were sighted. If the weather was unsuitable or low cloud exposed the boat to surprise attack, he was to abandon his approach. At night, attacks were to be pressed home regardless of enemy radar activity.

*　　*　　*

The German torpedo crisis at the beginning of the war has been well documented, but very little has been written about a long series of failures which were experienced with the acoustic torpedo of Type Zaunkönig. Yet these failures had far worse consequences. The crunch with the acoustic torpedo failures came in December and January when U972 (OL Klaus-Dietrich König) and U377 (OL Gerhard Kluth) sunk themselves with their own torpedoes. The Royal Navy picked up distress calls from two boats, which stated that they had been hit by torpedoes and went to investigate the matter and find out who had been responsible. The torpedoes had not been fired from an allied ship and there were no other U-boats in the vicinity, and so the Navy's operational intelligence in London concluded that the two U-boats had been victims of their own

acoustic torpedoes. For some years, it was thought that these distress calls had not been picked up by the German Navy and the U-boat Command had remained ignorant about the true fate of the boats. Signals were short and Otto Köhler (U377's first commander and a communications expert) and Wolfgang Hirschfeld (a U-boat and U-boat Command Radio Operator and author of a secret diary) both thought that it was easy to miss such messages, as a considerable number did not get through the first time they were transmitted. Yet, on examining the U-boat Command's war diary for 15 January 1944, there are details of U377's distress call: 'Emergency Report. Hit by torpedo. Boat heavily damaged and sinking'. The

Men from U48 demonstrating how the 20mm anti-aircraft gun was shot.

signature was missing and the time when it was received is not clear. The U-boat Command thought the message might have come from a German boat but that it was improbable because after a torpedo hit a U-boat it would be expected to sink immediately. This view of the signal's source is strange because it was transmitted in code Diana and any other source would suggest an intrusion into Germany's secret signalling system. Furthermore, a number of experienced radio operators thought that it was quite common for a distress call sent under such difficult conditions to be incomplete. It might have been coincidence, but on the same day Caution Signal No 80, which consisted of two orders regarding the use of torpedoes, was transmitted with details of new detonator adjustments.

In retrospect, it is easy to condemn the officers of the U-boat Command for having missed a vital piece of information, which might have led them to learn about the T5 failures, but it is doubtful whether an investigation would have pointed the finger at the German torpedoes and the assumption would have remained that they had been fired by the enemy, perhaps from another submarine. It might also be interesting to add that a few months earlier a Royal Navy commander made the blunder of transmitting details of his high frequency direction finder. The signal was decrypted by the German Radio Monitoring Service and appeared at the U-boat Command. Whether it was assumed to be simply referring to radar or was just overlooked is not known today, but officers responsible did not notice it until long after the war. When examining such cases of apparent negligence by the U-boat Command, it must be remembered that the staff were concerned principally with the day-to-day running of the U-boat war and had very little time for anything else. They did not have an intelligence department to support them and freely admit that it was impossible to read all the papers which appeared each day.

U377's classification, when it was lost, as an 'experienced and run-in' boat sheds an interesting light into what was considered as 'run-in'. U377 had been commissioned in 1941, but OL Gerhard Kluth was only on his second mission as commander, and he had been incapacitated due to wounds for most of his first voyage. The LI (Engineering Officer) was on his first mission without any supervision from a more experienced man; one of the diesel mechanics was new as were the radio operator, torpedo mechanic and Bootsmannsmaat responsible for the organisation in the central control room.

21. The Last of the Wolf Packs

March to May 1944

During the six months following September 1943, Dönitz made desperate efforts to regain a foothold in the important convoy war. First he thought that the acoustic torpedoes of Type Zaunkönig would make it possible to break through the ever strengthening escort screens, but he found his efforts blocked by aircraft. At first, this did not appear as a particularly serious setback; after all, the closure of the mid-Atlantic air gap had been predicted and, despite considerable delay, countermeasures were well under way. The other problem, the increasing number of aircraft in the Bay of Biscay which forced U-boats to remain submerged for long periods and so lengthened the time they required to reach their operations area, was thought to be solvable with the new anti-aircraft guns. The number of attacks on U-boats in the Biscay region had dropped drastically since radar warning devices had been introduced earlier in 1943, but the need to remain submerged meant two weeks were required to get in or out of a French port. Earlier it was possible to cross the coastal waters in two to four days.

Following the closure of the air gap, Dönitz decided that it might be better to avoid the long journey into mid-Atlantic and instead make an attempt to break through the convoy defences in the Western Approaches. In January 1944, two groups assembled on the European side of the Atlantic to test the U-boat Command's new theories of attacking on the surface. IGEL 1 consisted of 14 boats and IGEL 2 originally of eight, but was strengthened with another eight during the first week in February. The idea was that the boats be kept in loose formations and that they were only to pull themselves together in patrol lines when a convoy came close. Early on 8 February, U985 (KL Horst Kessler) managed to sink the 1735 GRT freighter *Margit* from convoy RA56, and another ten U-boats fired torpedoes. Several detonations were heard but nothing else was sunk during this hectic battle. The majority of the men considered themselves lucky to have escaped alive and the efforts and sacrifices made by boats of IGEL 1 and 2 demonstrated, quite clearly, that there was little hope of existing U-boat types regaining any sort of initiative in the North Atlantic. Exactly two years earlier, when U-boats were experiencing real success in American waters, Dönitz had been refused his request to increase the number

U802 (KL Helmut Schmoeckel) in Britain after the war. The raised navigation or sky periscope can be seen as well as a bracket and duct for the schnorkel.

of boats in the Atlantic. Now, when losses had reached epidemic proportions, he was being told by Hitler that the Atlantic was Germany's most important front and there could be no question of a withdrawal. There were two reasons for keeping U-boats in the Atlantic: to tie down enemy forces and to keep up-to-date with the latest enemy anti-submarine developments. To do the latter, in February 1944, it was decided to abandon wolf packs and to continue the war with independent boat operations.

Immediately after the war, a number of ex-U-boat men, led by Günter Hessler and Alfred Hoschatt, collaborated with the Royal Navy to write a thesis about the underwater war. The section dealing with attacks against U-boats is especially interesting because annotations by the Royal Navy indicate the German ignorance of British weapons. In addition to not knowing what the Allies were using against U-boats, by 1944 the German Navy had become paranoid about a variety of imaginary weapons. No one in the Kriegsmarine seems to have known what was happening at sea; how the enemy was finding and attacking U-boats; or how German weapons were behaving. To compound this ignorance, it was thought that the enemy used radio direction finders to locate U-boats and the independent boat operations led to further restrictions on transmissions from the sea. The majority of commanders did not transmit at all, thus cutting further the flow of information to the operations room.

Life in submarines had always been hectic, but now it was becoming severely strained. Often men had no idea what was hitting them. For example, boats thinking they were under attack from aircraft dived and then, when it was too late, realised the gunfire had come from a ship instead which had trapped them with Asdic. The next time, the commander might decide to remain on the surface, order torpedoes to be made ready and then find himself in a hail of bullets and depth charges from aircraft. Only about 35 percent of boats returned home and the few which did reported such varied experiences that it was often difficult to work out what had happened. U377 (OL Gerhard Kluth), for example, returned during October 1943 with a huge hole in the bows. This damage had almost proved fatal having missed one of the main ballast tanks by only a few centimetres. During the de-briefing, this encounter generated a heated discussion with Jumbo Gerke (U377's first watch officer, standing in for the seriously injured commander) being accused of having poor lookouts who did not spot a destroyer on a ramming course. Gerke's rejection of this suggestion was

Despite the war, domestic life had to continue and the provisioning of a boat with fuel and food was considered by many to be more important than the loading of torpedoes. Here, someone from U172 is collecting provisions from U530 in mid-Atlantic.

interrupted by someone looking at a photo of the boat showing scratches on the top of the conning tower. Eventually, both sides came to the conclusion that an aircraft had crashed on top of the diving boat. Yet, 20 years after the war, allied records indicate that fog kept all aircraft grounded that day and the problem has still not been satisfactorily solved.

February and March of 1944 saw an intensification of British air and submarine activity off Norway which led the German High Command into thinking an invasion might be imminent. Consequently, a special anti-invasion force, identified as Group MITTE, was established in northern waters. A short time later, a similar group was established in France under the name of LANDWIRT. While this was in progress, six lone boats were sent on sorties into enemy coastal waters. All experienced great difficulties but only

3 December 1945, Loch Ryan, Scotland. Type VIIC U-boats being prepared for scuttling during Operation Deadlight. U776 (KL Martin Lothar) surrendered in Weymouth, U281 (KL Heinrich von Davidson) in Kristiansand, U299 (OL Bernhard Emde) in Bergen and U369 (OL Hans-Norbert Schunck) in Kristiansand. The two raised periscopes have navigation lights attached. The one on the left is the attack periscope with a small top lens, and the one on the right the sky or navigation periscope. The eye piece of the first was in the commander's control room inside the conning tower and the other in the central control room, one deck lower; the attack periscope could be raised higher than the sky periscope. Round dipole aerials of radar detectors as well as 'periscopic' rod aerials can also be seen. U281 carries the insignia of U47, which was later adopted by other boats of the 7th U-Flotilla. The image of the snorting bull originated after U47's raid into Scapa Flow when the commander, KL Günter Prien reprimanded his Second Watch Officer for going for a walk along the upper deck and Amelung von Vahrendorf replied, 'Oh Herr Kaleu, but there is nothing going on in this empty bull fighting arena'. CPL

U35 under KK Werner Lott. The red and white rescue buoy with the light on the top, situated in the foreground on the deck, indicates that the photo was probably taken before the war. Water and oil filler caps were marked as can be seen on the side of the conning tower. It seems likely that the square with a cross indicated the fuel cap and the circular mark indicated water.

U24 (OL Helmut Hennig) off Königsberg in the Baltic.

U1003 (OL of the Reserve Werner Strübing), an Atlantic boat of Type VIIC in drydock. U1003 had to be scuttled after being grounded as a result of a collision with the Canadian frigate New Glasgow on 21 March 1945. The commander and about 15 of the crew lost their lives.

one, U744 (OL Heinz Blischke), was sunk, off Reykjavik. The other boats were U333 (KL Ali Cremer) and U586 (OL Hans Götze) in the North Channel; U413 (KL Gustav Poel) off Lizzard Point; U621 (OL Max Kruschka) in the Inner Hebrides; and U448 (OL Helmut Dauter) in Icelandic waters. This penetration of enemy waters was possible as a result of a new type of radar. Looking like a bedstead on the top of the conning tower and best known as Hohentwiel, it had a range of 15 to 20 kilometres against aircraft and could also detect the radar transmissions from enemy sets. The first operational tests in U311 (KL Joachim Zander) and U743 (OL Helmut Kandzior) were especially encouraging because the device made it possible to range guns before attacking aircraft came into sight. This made for a quieter routine which was considerably less stressful for the men. The appearance of Hohentwiel coincided with the introduction of schnorkels for running diesel engines below the surface. Availability of the air masts could not meet demand because air attacks on the manufacturing plants as well as on transport routes delayed their arrival at the French bases.

U264 (KL Hartwig Looks), the first operational boat with a schnorkel, was lost on 19 February without having sent an evaluation report. Although the second boat, U575 (OL Wolfgang

Boehmer), managed to broadcast a brief account before being sunk, it was not until the middle of May that the first positive assessment could be made. On the nineteenth, U667 (KL Heinrich Schroeteler) returned to France having remained submerged for almost ten days. The following day, U267 (KL Otto Tinschert) arrived to make further reports. Both men thought it would be beneficial to learn the tricks of the new invention away from the battle front and special training facilities were established in Norway.

While Hohentwiel radar and schnorkels were making their mark, the Royal Air Force continued to intensify its efforts in the Bay of Biscay. German radar detectors, and the U-boats' new procedures of remaining submerged for much of their passage through the Black Pit, had reduced the U-boat casualties. On the other hand the RAF's efforts were increased and their daring was clearly demonstrated on 25 March, when a number of Mosquitoes sunk U976 (KL Raimund Tiesler) close to the harbour in St Nazaire. Four weeks later a similar attack against U255 (OL Erich Harms) highlighted Germany's inability to protect her front door. Even the usually quiet waters off Norway saw a new phase of interference from aircraft. U476 (OL Otto Niethmann) had to be abandoned after damage sustained while shooting down a Liberator and the rescuing U-boat, U990 (KL Hubert Nordheimer), was lost in a similar duel during the following day.

In February 1943, Rodger Winn (head of the submarine tracking room at the Admiralty in London) predicted morale would suffer badly once the U-boat losses reached 10 percent of the boats at sea and he suggested there might be a considerable slowing down of the U-boat offensive once losses rose to 15 percent. Yet, a year later, sinkings had reached the far more alarming figure of nearer 70 percent and U-boats still continued to sail principally because of bad German intelligence. For example, Dönitz told his men that it was thought that the enemy was employing 1500 aircraft against them and he maintained that these would be unleashed against Germany if U-boats vacated the Atlantic. In *The War at Sea*, Captain S W Roskill gives the following figures for January 1944: 50 very long-range aircraft, 70 long-range, 280 medium-range and 110 flying boats; making a total of 510. Quite a proportion of these would have been unsuitable for employment against land targets, but the German High Command reckoned that their crews were trained to fight over water and could have been sent out to disrupt vital coastal traffic once the Allies no longer required them over the waters to the west of Britain.

22. Operations in Remote Areas

Following the disastrous losses of May 1943, boats with sufficient fuel were ordered south to the Azores into the only area where they could still be employed with a faint glimmer of hope. There, 16 boats formed a patrol line under the name of TRUTZ. Three of them at the end of the line came under attack from carrier borne aircraft, but merchant ships were not sighted. Finally, when they gathered around the U-tanker, U488 (OL Erwin Bartke), the outward-bound U758 (KL Helmut Manseck) stumbled upon a group of merchant ships sailing through the area where Group TRUTZ had just been. TRUTZ continued to operate for some time and, in the end, the formation was moved eastwards, towards Spain where the boats received the identification of Group GEIER. The fruitless effort of hunting convoys off the Azores was eventually abandoned. Five U-boats had been lost but not a single merchant ship sunk.

March 1943 to March 1944

The failures with TRUTZ and GEIER led Dönitz to try his luck in more far-flung fringes of the Atlantic. Initially, the plan which sent boats along the American and African coasts produced much better results. Commanders concentrated on focal points in merchant routes and they were given enough freedom to cover wide areas. Radio transmissions were kept to an absolute minimum, and even the usual practice of sending position reports was abandoned. Consequently, the secret submarine tracking room at the Admiralty in London had problems in determining exact positions. However, once sighted, boats were pursued with the usual vigour and operations were eventually frustrated by air attacks. A few commanders found the intensity of the attacks to be as strong and persistent as in the Bay of Biscay.

These U-boat operations on the fringes of the Atlantic started hurriedly, while support facilities were still not ready. U-tankers were still being fitted out when U-boats were already under way and they followed a short distance behind. During earlier undertakings U-tankers had usually been dispatched ahead of fighting boats so that refuelling could take place before the commencement of action. This had the advantage that boats would still have enough fuel to return home, if they failed to meet the supply boat. Furthermore, damaged boats could start the long and hazardous return journey without having to seek out the supply vessel. Now, that strategy

Crew wearing underwater escape apparatus, which could be inflated and used as a lifebelt, on the bows of U172 (KK Carl Emmermann) with the sinking U604 (KL Horst Höltring) in the background. Höltring and about half his crew were rescued by U185 (KL August Maus), which was lost with all hands before landing the survivors from U604. The device sticking up from the deck is the head of underwater sound detection equipment and the ring, in front of it, is the socket to hold the capstan.

was reversed and frontline boats found themselves virtually exhausted and in need of the extra fuel and supplies before they could set off for home.

Royal Navy intelligence might have had problems tracking a relatively few number over the wide areas, but the positions of the supply locations, broadcast to U-boats at sea, made it easy to pin-point the secret meeting places. The results were predictable: destroyers or aircraft were sent out to concentrate on the vulnerable supply boats. U459 (KK Georg von Wilamowitz-Moellendorf), due to be positioned 600 miles east of Bermuda to refuel Caribbean boats; U462 (OL Bruno Vowe) due 400 miles west of the Cape Verde Islands for boats from South America, and their reserve, U461 (KK Wolf Stiebler), were lost before any of them reached their secret destinations. The other supply boats, U489 (OL Adalbert Schmandt) and U117 (KK Hans Werner Neumann), a mine-layer of Type XB, could not be diverted because African front boats were relying on them. To make matters worse in the west, a rescue

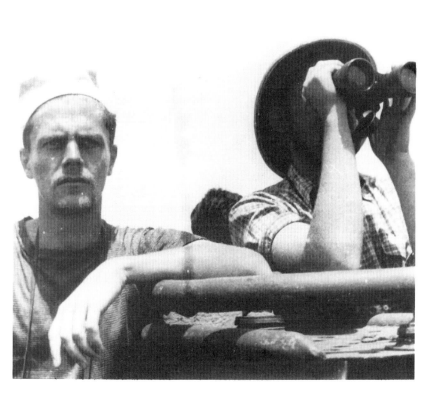

KK Carl Emmermann (U172) on the left, August 1943. At the time of this photograph, Emmermann had little to smile about, finding himself probably in one of the most difficult periods of his command. Together with U185 (KL August Maus) he picked up the crew of the sinking U604 (KL Horst Höltring) and U172 only just managed to reach home. U185 was lost. There were no survivors.

operation had to be mounted to save the crew of U604 (KL Horst Höltring), which was seriously damaged by depth charges from USS *Moffet*. U172 (KL Carl Emmermann) and U185 (KL August Maus) found the area saturated with aircraft. On 11 August, while such valuable items such as food were being removed from the stricken boat, a Liberator was shot down in a ball of fire during which Horst Höltring was seriously injured. He died shortly afterwards from his wounds.

Meanwhile, boats on the eastern side of the Atlantic were faring no better. U66 (KL Friedrich Markworth) reported having been attacked by carrier borne aircraft and that they were having problems locating U117. A short time later, after U84 (KL Horst Uphoff) had sighted two destroyers at the secret refuelling location, it became obvious that the supply boat had been sunk. The 14 African boats realised they were in greater trouble than expected. U571 (OL Gustav Lüssow), U600 (KL Bernhard Zurmühlen) and U618 (OL Erich Faust), all of them Type VIIC boats, had no chance of getting home without fuel and U129 (a Type IXC under OL Richard von Harpe) had to be diverted to rescue them. The long-distance boat, U847 (KL Herbert Kuppisch), was told to help U172 and U185. None of these vessels carried fuel pipes and oil had to be pumped over in fire hoses. U185 had already been sunk, U847 was lost a week later and only U172 succeeded in returning to France, demonstrating that even the far off regions had become untenable. The end of supply missions was acknowledged in October when U220 (OL Bruno Barber) and U460 (KL Ebe Schnoor) were lost. The first mentioned was a large mine-layer of Type XB and not a purpose-built submarine supply boat like U460, but this type had a large enough capacity and was often used to provision other boats.

The introduction of new radar equipment during the summer of 1943 was followed by a brief period in which it appeared as if U-boats had again found better prospects, and in October 1943 another thrust was planned into more distant waters. This time Dönitz planned to mine key traffic junctions in the western Atlantic. Two Type XB, U103 (KL Gustav-Adolf Janssen) and U220 (OL Bruno Barber), and two Type VIID, U214 (OL Gerhard Conrad) and U218 (KL Rupprecht Stock) were sent to Takoradi, St Johns, Colon and Trinidad. At the same time, U68 (OL Albert Lauzemis) and U515 (KL Werner Henke) went into the Gulf of Guinea with mines, and U516 (KL Hans-Rutger Tillessen) into the Caribbean. On reaching the approaches to the Panama Canal, Tillessen stirred up such rigourous opposition that he had great difficulty in withdrawing again. The B-Dienst supplied the U-boat Command with the constant stream of enemy sighting reports and after a couple of days, Tillessen was given permission to divert anywhere he liked until the hunt had died down, and he was promised that fuel would be dispatched to ensure he had enough to get home. Once again, the U-boat Command offered the Allies an excellent means of finding a target. U544 (KL Willy Mattke), a Type IXC boat, moved into a secret rendezvous to refuel while U129 (OL Richard von Harpe) converged on the spot with much needed radar equipment for U516. Detonations were heard close to the meeting point and U544 did not show up as planned. It had been sunk by carrier borne aircraft from USS *Guadalcanal* and U539 (KL Hans-Jürgen Lauterbach-Emden) had to be diverted to refuel U516. These incidents caused the U-boat Command to re-examine their radio procedures yet again. Günter Hessler states that the assurances given in 1941 about the security of the naval code were never fully believed. Yet there was no real evidence to suggest that the code was

The upper foredeck of U68 (KK Karl-Friedrich Merten) with men taking the opportunity to exercise. The gun is of 105mm calibre and this photograph illustrates the characteristic wide upper deck of Types IX.

Some insignia were fully functional. This swastika on U181 was there to help identification and prevent accidental attack by friendly Japanese forces.

being compromised and, again, nothing was done to find the cause of the sinkings of so many supply ships at the critical moment of transferring provisions. Today, it is difficult to understand Germany's apparently complacent attitude towards the security problems.

* * *

Boats of the long-distance MONSOON Group, which left France for the Far East between March and May, reported similar experiences to those of the boats along the western fringes of the Atlantic. The project got off to a bad start when the supply ships were sunk before they reached the South Atlantic and operations in the Indian Ocean could only go ahead after *Charlotte Schliemann* was sent out from Japan to meet the U-boats heading east. This Hamburg-based tanker had been marooned in the Far East since the beginning of the war and had served as a supply ship for surface raiders. She had then stayed in Japanese controlled waters. Her presence in the Indian Ocean during June 1943 made it possible for the U-boats to reap a surprisingly good harvest there. Some of the MONSOON boats

A crewman of U181 dressed in rain gear with uninflated life jacket and improvised safety line, using a T spanner to tighten nuts on the upper deck.

headed further east and established Penang as the first Oriental German submarine base. The others made the return journey to France. U197 (KL Robert Bartels) reported being damaged by aircraft while rounding The Cape and U181 (KK Wolfgang Lüth) and U196 (OL Werner Striegler) went to his assistance, but found no survivors. Incidentally, these last two remained at sea for record periods of time. U196 was at sea for 217 days or 31 weeks while under command of KK Eitel-Friedrich Kentrat and U181 for 206 days under KK Wolfgang Lüth. The loss of U197 was followed by a noticeable increase in allied activity in both the South Atlantic and Indian Ocean, and some commanders came to regard those areas as more treacherous than the Black Pit of Biscay.

Activity in the Indian Ocean depended on the presence of a supply ship and *Charlotte Schliemann* returned to a lonely spot, some 100 miles southeast of Mauritius to refuel U178 (KL Wilhelm Spahr) and U510 (KL Alfred Eick), both homeward-bound from Penang. U178 had been the first U-boat to arrive in Penang and her commander, KK Wilhelm Dommes remained there to organise the setting up of the German submarine base. Wilhelm Spahr started the war as Obersteuermann in U47, under Günter Prien, and had

U161, a Type IXC from the small Seebeckwerft in Wesermünde (now Bremerhaven). The boat was commissioned by Hans Ludwig Witt and later commanded by Albrecht Achilles, who went down with it in September 1943.

A Type VIIA in drydock. This was the only U-boat type of World War II with an above-water torpedo tube, clearly seen on the stern.

travelled out to the Far East as U181's First Watch Officer. Following the refuelling Spahr continued his voyage to Bordeaux, while Eick remained for a while in the hope of sinking a few ships before resuming his journey for France. Two weeks later U532 (FK Ottoheinrich Junker), another homeward-bound boat from Penang made contact with the tanker, but bad weather delayed the refuelling. They lost sight of each other during the storm and afterwards, harried by long-range flying boats, U532 was unable to make contact again with the tanker. The Royal Navy, aware of the *Charlotte Schliemann*, sent the cruiser *Newcastle* and destroyer *Relentless* with air support to sink it. *Newcastle* ran short of fuel before the task could be accomplished but the *Relentless* succeeded in sinking the tanker shortly before running low on fuel itself.

U532, although classed as a long-range version of Type IXC, did not compare with the very long-range boats of Type IXD2. The latter could cover a maximum of 32,300 nautical miles (almost 60,000 kilometres), but U532 was limited to half that distance and the loss of *Charlotte Schliemann* was a grave blow for it. U178 transferred what fuel could be spared and then U532 just had to wait for the next wave of U-boats which was under way from the Far East and making for Europe in company with the tanker *Brake*. This time a new strategy was tried out. U168 (KL Helmuth Pich), U188 (KL Siegfried Lüdden) and U532 (FK Ottoheinrich Junker) scoured the area to check for anti-submarine patrols and, having found no signs of any, converged on the tanker to refuel. This time, bad weather prevented the Royal Navy from putting in an appearance and U188 and U532 were supplied without interference, albeit under the most difficult conditions. On disengaging from the tanker though, planes were spotted by lookouts onboard U188 and though it was able to dive and evade the attack *Brake* was sunk. Later, U188 and U168 picked up survivors.

Hessler and Hoschatt regarded the loss of another tanker, in the same area in which the *Charlotte Schliemann* was sunk, as remarkable, especially as the position was a long way from both air and naval bases. Once again, the finger was pointed at Germany's radio code, but the Supreme Naval Command suggested that U-boat sightings had led the Allies to the the tankers. The radio code was examined again, but no definite conclusions could be drawn from the available evidence. In March 1944, Hessler received the news that U488 (OL Bruno Studt), the last supply boat of Type XIV, had been lost and commented, 'these are painful and unnecessary losses'.

23. The Final Struggle

The German High Command held the view that an allied invasion of the European continent could only be defeated by land forces and the long chain of concrete coastal installations remains as a reminder of the effort which was put into this defence. The mass of concrete was necessary because a large proportion of Germany's armed forces, as well as virtually all the modern mobile equipment was in the east, fighting the Russians. The small naval lobby in Hitler's headquarters could do very little in the way of preparing to frustrate an allied onslaught, other than make arrangements for U-boats to be assembled in Norway and France standing by at six hours' notice to go to sea against an invasion force. It had already been demonstrated that U-boats could not tackle the enemy in the vastness of the Atlantic and Rodger Winn (head of the secret submarine tracking room in London) confidently told the Admiralty that U-boats were powerless within a 400-mile radius of a well trained anti-submarine group.

By the time that the anti-invasion groups were being assembled, the U-boat Command had acknowledged the inferiority of the new anti-aircraft armament. The 37mm automatic did not live up to its expectations. Shoddy workmanship coupled with inferior materials led to too many failures at critical moments and boats surfaced only for short periods when it was dark making maintenance work most difficult. Anti-aircraft rockets, which were tried out in February by U986 (OL Karl-Ernst Kaiser) did not achieve any significant results.

Although schnorkels have often been hailed as the saviours in an hour of need, they actually created more problems than they solved. Commanders were told to stop engines at least once every half hour to sweep with their sound detection gear, but there was no advice as to what to do if they were detected. In the Atlantic, navigational errors often resulted from remaining submerged for long periods and schnorkelling under cloudy skies. This had one positive side effect in that the positions, picked up by the Allies, were often wrong. Once within the tidal currents of the English Channel, however, this inaccuracy became a serious problem.

The sort of navigational difficulties that arose are well illustrated by the experiences of U763 (KL Ernst Cordes). Having drifted for some time, without being able to establish his position, Cordes took

a bearing on the Brest radio transmitter and reckoned his position to be somewhere near the Channel Islands. Surfacing at night, with the view of getting an accurate fix, he noticed land on two sides of the boat and realised that U763 was on the other side of the English Channel at Spithead, the Royal Navy anchorage between the Isle of Wight and Portsmouth. He had accidentally performed what had been thought to be impossible. There were no large targets and Cordes did not particularly want to draw attention to his plight by attacking small boats. Neither did he want to run the risk of possibly beaching a LUT or T5 torpedo, so he concentrated on extricating himself from this vulnerable position. After hearing Cordes' report, the U-boat Command made plans to send a mine-layer there, but these thoughts were interrupted by the evacuation of the French bases.

Since little was known about the Channel and the last major shallow water operations were carried out off America during the first months of 1942, an exploratory, dress rehearsal thrust was ordered for schnorkel boats of the anti-invasion group. As it happened, this took place just a few weeks before D-Day. The five-boat DRAGONER Group returned from the north of Quessant not only with valuable schnorkelling experience but also with the chilling suspicion that enemy airborne radar was capable of detecting boats when only the schnorkel head valve showed above the

Guns have not yet been fitted to the post-1942 platform shown here. A schnorkel is in place and the fitting of four pressure-resistant containers for rubber dinghies suggests that this photograph was taken after the summer of 1944. It could have been taken after the war, when the boat was on its way to Britain, prior to being sunk during Operation Deadlight. It could be U930 (OLdR Kurt Mohr).

Two of the small electro coastal boats which were put into service towards the end of the war. U2336 (KL Emil Klausmeier) was built at Deutsche Werft in Hamburg and surrendered in Kiel at the end of the war.

A close-up of the schnorkel valve gear of U1109. It has been covered with rubber to help absorb radar impulses and the circular dipole aerial of a radar detector can be seen. The valve gear differed considerably, with several different designs having been produced during the short period when schnorkels were in use.

water. These suspicions had hardly been digested when, at 0300 hours on 6 June, news of the Normandy landings activated the U-boat Command's operations room. For the past six months it had been in a new bunker some 20 miles from Berlin. Code named *Koralle*, the complex was situated near the village of Bernau to the northeast of the capital.

Konteradmiral Eberhard Godt (chief of the U-boat Command) ordered non-schnorkel boats of a group on passage from Norway to France to remain where they were and those with schnorkels to continue at fast speed. Seven of the eight schnorkel boats in Brest were put on alert and ordered to leave as soon as they were ready. Then he sat back, telling his staff all immediate action had been taken. Instructions for the other boats were withheld. His reasoning was that the invasion would bring an intensification of anti-U-boat activity and that there was no point in deploying non-schnorkel boats against such unfair odds. In the U-boat Command's diary, Godt emphasised the need to keep boats in reserve to meet landings in other locations. Not being aware of Mulberry harbours, the large concrete pontoons towed across the Channel and sunk to convert open beaches into unloading areas, Godt expected ports to come under attack once the enemy required more dock facilities.

A few hours later, Dönitz ordered Godt to send all boats from the French bases to sea, making it plain they were to go into the English Channel. Dönitz said, 'They have to be engaged regardless of cost because the outcome of this invasion is going to be the most decisive factor of the whole war'. Recent events had shown that it was impossible for the U-boats without schnorkels to get anywhere near the enemy in the vastness of the Atlantic. In fact, operations had become so difficult that only a few weeks earlier the U-boat Command had restricted boats to a maximum of eight weeks at sea and all of them were sent into the Atlantic fitted with the latest radar, a radar detector and schnorkel. Now, when Godt was ordered to go against his better judgement, despite so many devastating experiences in recent months, he wrote in the U-boat Command's diary, 'This means boats without schnorkels are being sent on their last missions'. Günter Hessler said that Dönitz was forced into ordering the non-schnorkel boats into the Channel. Whatever the origin of the order, Godt did not carry it out. Instead, he positioned the boats in what he called a reconnaissance veil across the Bay of Biscay and argued that they would be ready to repel a possible thrust against the French Atlantic bases.

The decision to send schnorkel boats to the invasion area with all

U875 (KL Georg Preuss) in Northern Ireland after the war, showing schnorkel, navigation or sky periscope and attack periscope raised. Keeping lookout while schnorkelling was not easy because the motion usually caused the periscopes to vibrate. A stabiliser has been fitted to this long-range boat of Type IXD2. Both periscopes of Types IX terminated in the commander's control room inside the conning tower, making it possible to extend both to the same height. On a Type VII the attack periscope could only be used from the conning tower room and the other one from the central control room, one deck lower down.

The schnorkel and two periscopes of U516 (OL Friedrich Petran), a Type IXC/ 40. The different sizes of the head lenses are clearly visible. The attack periscope, with the smaller lens, is on the right. Note that there was a radar detection aerial on the top of the conning tower and on the schnorkel.

possible speed, on the surface at night, had to be abandoned after nine air attacks on six boats in a few hours of the first night. German leaders in Berlin appeared to be quite out of touch with reality and unaware of the strength of anti-U-boat forces. Indeed, the allied efforts to prevent U-boats reaching the most vulnerable supply lines seem to have been under-estimated. Operation Cork, intended to block off the western approaches to the Channel by flying intensive anti-submarine patrols, was a great success for the Royal Air Force. On the third night, only two boats of the first wave (U740, KL Günther Stark and U821, OL Ulrich Knackfuss) were still at sea. They were advised to return to Brest, but fell victims to aircraft before reaching their concrete protection. Few U-boats found targets and a number of those which did were rewarded with dud torpedoes. OL Hermann Stuckmann (U621), for example, heard the premature explosions of a complete salvo. He was awarded the Knights Cross, perhaps in compensation, but a week later he went down with his boat.

Following the initial period of intensity during the invasion, there followed a period of calm for the U-boat Command. The relief of knowing that nothing could be contributed by sacrificing more boats in the Channel gave way to looking for alternative ways of taking the pressure off Normandy. The suggestion that non-schnorkel boats might be sent out into the Atlantic as a diversion force did not find much favour. The majority of officers argued that the enemy had sufficient forces without having to divert any from the Channel and that ordering the U-boats into the Atlantic would amount to nothing more than suicide missions.

The rapid developments at the front and fears of a breakdown in communications between the U-boat Command near Berlin and France led to the F.d.U. West (Füherer der Unterseeboote West; Flag Officer for Submarines – KS Hans Rösing) being given more operational control of boats in his area. The position of F.d.U. had been created in 1942 to co-ordinate the administration network on the Atlantic coast. In early August, a week after this change in the leadership pattern, the American breakout from the consolidated beachhead threatened Brest, Lorient and St Nazaire. The Germans did not anticipate the allied plans to avoid large towns and thus prepared to defend them until serviceable boats, valuable equipment and key personnel could be moved out. Boats being sent out to sea and those already there were told to reckon with the closing of the northern French bases and thus allow enough fuel for running to Bordeaux or Norway.

Spare parts, especially new schnorkels, non-ferrous metals and skilled dockyard workers were to be moved out of the three ports under threat. This monumental undertaking with overladen boats was made even more precarious by the presence of the Royal Navy which had virtual free run of the French coastal waters. Losses, which were pretty well evenly divided between schnorkel and non-schnorkel boats led the U-boat Command to assume that the majority had been sunk by mines. The advancing American Army forced Hans Rösing to move his headquarters from Angers to La Pallice and in Brest flotilla chiefs set about the destruction of important documents. Retreating soldiers, gathering in the coastal towns to seek shelter in U-boat bunkers, added to an atmosphere of confusion and led to a partial breakdown in discipline. Seaworthy boats had left by the time the Germans realised that the allied armies were by-passing the Atlantic ports. This news was followed by an attempt to re-supply Lorient and St Nazaire with necessities which had been disposed of earlier. U445 (OL Rupprecht Fischler Graf von Treuberg) and U650 (OL Rudolf Zorn) left La Pallice on 12 August to return to Lorient as cargo carriers. The loading of U180

A Type XXI boat in Heikendorfer Bay near the U-boat Memorial at Möltenort (Kiel).

(OL Rolf Riesen) and U195 (OL Friedrich Steinfeldt) in Bordeaux was held up by a shortage of supplies and both boats were prevented from sailing when it was discovered they carried some miscellaneous cargo plus several tons of seawater ballast.

The crews of boats which could not be made ready in time were carried to Norway as passengers in other U-boats, ordered to make their way overland to Germany or drafted into land defence forces. The overland trek was by far the most dangerous, with many small bands of ill-equipped men falling easy prey to allied forces or to bands of the French underground. A number of boats which left France towards the end of August managed to reach Norway without serious incidents and only one (U445, OL Rupprecht Fischler Graf von Treuberg) of the last wave was lost. The last boat out of France, U267 (OL Bernhard Knieper) left on 23 September and arrived in Norway after a passage of five weeks.

*   *   *

Having evacuated the French bases, only a few die-hards believed in the plans for re-grouping in Norway for another major onslaught with the new electro boats. Most knew that there was no hope and that it was now simply a matter of survival. As the Battle of the Atlantic drew to a close, a few isolated operations continued in Canadian and American waters while the majority of crews made an effort to remain alive in British coastal waters and on the eastern side of the Atlantic. Following the fall of France, another hundred or so U-boats were lost to anti-submarine forces, but only a small harvest was reaped for this sacrifice. Although this phase has usually been regarded as the Kriegsmarine's last stand, the German Navy's biggest battle had not yet taken place. Towards the end of 1944, most of the action shifted into the Baltic where every vessel with fuel was used to evacuate refugees from the east under most difficult circumstances. Several ships with thousands of people on board – *Wilhelm Gustloff* with over 5000, *Goya* with 6500, *General* V *Steuben* with 2700 – were sunk and by comparison the casualties during the Battle for the Atlantic look small.

The Interior of an Atlantic U-Boat

The bow torpedo compartment of U889. The torpedo adjusting device for anti-convoy looping torpedoes can be seen between the four torpedo tubes. Information from the bridge and the conning tower control room was transmitted to this machine and range, course and speed of convoy indicated on dials. The settings of the torpedoes already in the tubes could be adjusted by turning knobs which rotated another set of indicators and everything was ready to fire when the two were lined up. Although the torpedoes could be fired from the bridge, most commanders insisted that the torpedo mechanic pressed his firing button when the order was given. CPL

The central control room of U889, looking forward. The rudder controls can be seen at the bottom, to the right of the circular pressure-resistant door. The two buttons on the top moved the rudder to the right or left. Above it, in a black casing, is a repeater from the girocompass and above that are two engine indicators. Above these is a small black-looking screen which showed the position of the magnetic compass, which was situated outside the pressure hull, at the base of the conning tower. A voice pipe going up to the commander's control room in the conning tower and to the bridge can be seen. A depth gauge and part of the manual hydroplane controls are just visible on the right. Towards the left are two boxes numbered 3 and 4. These could be parts of automatic depth keeping gear. CPL

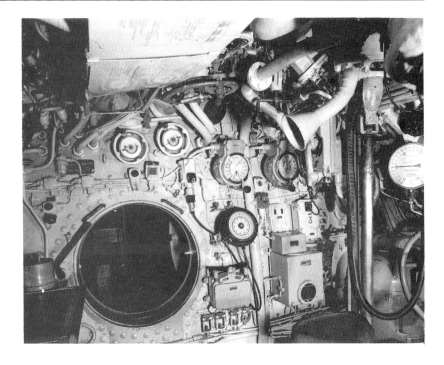

The central control room looking aft. Note that the voice pipe in the foreground can be seen in the picture above. The ladder up the conning tower can be seen with the housing for the attack periscope. On the left are the trim controls and on the right the chart table. The pole coming down from the ceiling, just to the left of the chart table, is the bottom part of the Hohentwiel radar and radar detection device. CPL

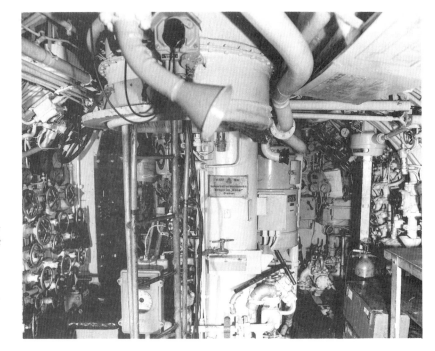

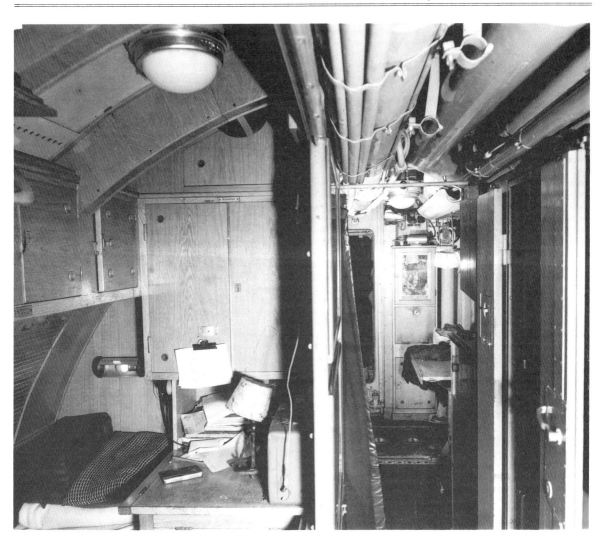

The commander's cabin on the left and the radio room on the right, looking forward. 'Cabin' is not really a good description. The commander had only a bunk and table and a heavy curtain with which to shut himself off. CPL

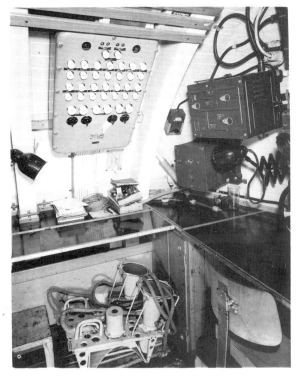

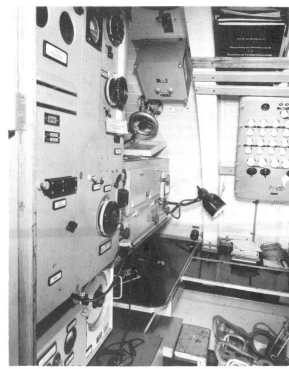

The radio room of U889, looking slightly forwards. The gadget on the floor is of particular interest. It is a radar aerial of Type Tunis. Two devices, a radar set and a radar detector, known respectively as Type Fliege and Type Mücke were fitted into the one apparatus. The panel with the white knobs is a fuse box. CPL

The controls at the back of the radio compartment. The cupboard at the bottom was used to accommodate the secret code writer. CPL

*The diesel compartment,
looking aft. At the far end is a
door leading to the electro
room and in front of that, in the
middle, the aft hatch. This was
usually not used at sea.* CPL

*The controls of the electro
room looking aft.* CPL

The after torpedo compartment and accommodation for the crew. Two torpedoes are still lying on the floor and a single beam with winches could be slid from side to side for lifting torpedoes into the tubes. The wires hanging down were used for attaching bunk-like hammocks.

One of the pressure-resistant doors of the petty officers' room.

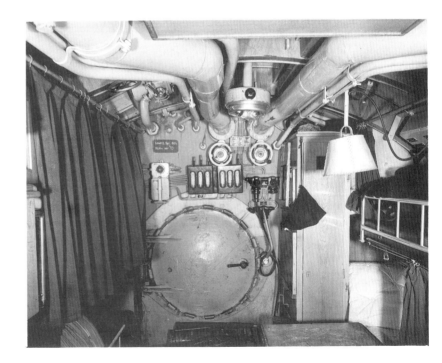

Select Bibliography

Beaver, Paul, *U-boats in the Atlantic*, Patrick Stephens Ltd, Cambridge, 1979. (Good photographs from the German Federal Archive.)

Bekker, Cajus, *Hitler's Naval War*, Macdonald and Jane's, London, 1974

Bödeker, Günter, *Die Boote im Netz*, Gustav Lübbe Verlag, Bergisch Gladbach, 1981

Bonatz, Heinz, *Seekrieg im Äther*, E S Mittler & Sohn, Herford, 1981. (The author commanded the German Naval Radio Monitoring Service during the war.)

Brennecke, Jochen, *Jäger Gejagte*, Köhlers Verlagsgesellschaft, Herford, 1956.

Brennecke, Jochen, *Die Wende im U-boot-Krieg*, Köhlers Verlagsgesellschaft, Herford, 1984.

Busch, Harald, *So war der U-bootskrieg*, Deutsche Heimat Verlag, Bielefeld, 1954. (The author served aboard U-boats as war correspondent. A good book.)

Compton-Hall, Richard, *The Underwater War 1939–45*, Blandford, Poole, 1982. (The author is the Director of the Royal Navy's Submarine Museum and this is an excellent account about life in submarines and how they operated.)

Deutscher Marinebund: Ubootsmuseum U995; Laboe. (A guide book to the U-boat by the German Naval Memorial.)

Deutscher Marinebund: Dönitz, DMB, Wilhelmshaven, 1981.

Dönitz, Karl, *Zehn Jahre und Zwanzig Tage*, Athenäum Verlag, Bonn, 1958.

Dönitz, Karl *Mein wechselvolles Leben*, Musterschmidt Verlag, Frankfurt, 1968.

Dönitz, Karl, *Deutsche Strategie zur See im zweiten Weltkrieg*, Bernard & Graefe, Frankfurt, 1972. (The answers to forty questions put by journalists.)

Dönitz, Karl, *Die U-bootswaffe*, E S Mittler Verlag, Berlin, 1939.

Erskine, Ralph, 'U-boats, Homing Signals and HFDF'. (A brief article in Vol 2 No 2 of *Intelligence and National Security*, Frank Cass, London, 1987.)

Gabler, Ulrich, *Unterseebootsbau*, Wehr und Wissen Verlagsgesellschaft, Darmstadt, 1964. (The author worked with Prof Helmuth Walter on electro submarines and after the war became director of a famous submarine construction bureau.)

Giese, Fritz, *Die deutsche Marine 1920–45*, Bernard & Graefe, Frankfurt, 1956.

Giessler, Helmuth, *Der Marine-Nachrichten und Ortungsdienst*, J F Lehmanns Verlag, Munich 1971.

Gretton, Peter, *Convoy Escort Commander*, Cassell, London, 1964. (The author served as escort commander during the war.)

Gröner, Erich, *Die deutschen Kriegsschiffe 1815–1945*, Vol 3, Bernard & Graefe, Koblenz, 1985.

Hadley, Michael *U-boats against Canada*, McGill-Queen's University Press, Kingston and Montreal, 1985. (An excellent account.)

Hering, Robert, *Chronik der Crew 37a*, Hering, Gärtringen. (An excellent set of records, published privately.)

Herwig, Holger H, *Das Elitekorps des Kaisers*, H Christians Verlag, Hamburg, 1977.

Herzog, Bodo, *60 Jahre deutsche Uboote 1906–1966*, J F Lehmanns Verlag, Munich, 1968. (A useful book with much tabulated information and interesting photos.)

Herzog, Bodo, *U-boats in Action*, Ian Allan, Weybridge, 1971. (A pictorial book with captions in German and English. Most interesting.)

Hirschfeld, Wolfgang, *Feindfahrten*, Neff Verlag, Vienna, 1982. (The author served as radio operator in U109, U234 and at the U-boat Command and this is his secret diary. This is one of the best and most valuable wartime reports on the U-boat war.)

Högel, Georg, *Embleme, Wappen, Malings deutscher Uboote 1939–45*, Koehlers, Herford, 1987. (A very good book about emblems painted on U-boat conning towers.)

Hoffmann, Rudolf, *50 Jahre Olympia Crew*, published privately in 1986. (An excellent account.)

Jones, Geoff, *The Months of the Lost U-boats*, William Kimber, London, 1977. (About May 1943.)

Jones, Geoff, *Autumn of the U-boats*, William Kimber, London, 1984. (About the autumn of 1943.)

Jones, Geoff, *Defeat of the Wolf Packs*, William Kimber, London, 1986. (About the end of wolf pack operations in early 1944.)

Kludas, Arnold: *Technikmuseum Uboot Wilhelm Bauer*, Bremerhaven, 1985. (A guide to the museum.)

Koop, Gerhard & Mulitze, Erich, *Die Marine in Wilhelmshaven*, Bernard & Graefe Verlag, Koblenz, 1987. (Contains 350 interesting photographs, most of which have not previously been published.)

Lohmann, W & Hildebrand, H H, *Kriegsmarine 1939–45*, Podzun Verlag, Dorheim 1956–64. (This is the standard work giving details of naval organisation in three volumes.)

Lüdde-Neurath, Walter, *Regierung Dönitz*, Musterschmidt, Göttingen, 1964. (About the last days of the Dönitz government. The author was Dönitz's last adjutant.)

Miller, Ian A, *The Tempest and various publications by Sons and Daughters of United States Merchant Mariners of World War II*, 1806 Bantry Trail, Kernersville, NC 27284, USA.

Milner, Marc, *North Atlantic Run*, Naval Institute Press, 1985.

Morison, Samuel Eliot, *History of United States Naval Operations in World War II*, Little, Brown and Co, Boston, 1970. (This is supposed to be the official US history of the war and the author is reputed to have had access to wartime records.)

National Archives and Records Administration, *Records Relating to U-boat Warfare 1939–45*, Washington DC, 1985. (An excellent catalogue of German records.)

Porten, Edward von der, *The German Navy in World War II*, Arthur Baker Ltd, London, 1969.

Prochnow, Günther, *Deutsche Kriegsschiffe in zwei Jahrhunderten*, Vol IV, Unterseeboote; Ernst Gades Verlag, Preezt, 1969. (A good small book giving mechanical details and the fate of each boat.)

Raeder, Dr Erich, *My Life*, US Naval Institute, 1960.

Raeder, Dr Erich, *Struggle for the Sea*, William Kimber, London, 1959.

Rohwer, Dr Prof Jürgen, *Uboote – Eine Chronik in Bildern*, Gerhard Stalling Verlag, Oldenburg, 1962.

Rohwer, Dr Prof Jürgen, *U107*, Profile Publications, Windsor, 1971.

Rohwer, Dr Prof Jürgen, *Axis Submarine Successes 1939–45*, Patrick Stephens, Cambridge, 1983.

Rohwer, Dr Prof Jürgen, *The Critical Convoy Battles of March 1943*, Ian Allan, Weybridge, 1977.

Rohwer, Dr Prof Jürgen and Hümmelchen, Gerhard, *Chronology of the War at Sea*, Ian Allan, Weybridge 1977. (Two volumes.)

Rohwer, Dr Prof Jürgen and Jäckel, Eberhard, *Die Funkaufklärung und ihre Rolle im 2. Weltkrieg*, Motorbuch Verlag, Stuttgart, 1979.

Roskill, Captain S W, *The War at Sea*, HMSO, London, 1954 and 1976. (The official British history in four volumes.)

Roskill, Captain S W, *The Secret Capture*, Collins, London, 1959. (About the capture of U110 Kl Fritz-Julius Lemp.)

Rössler, Eberhard, *Geschichte des deutschen Ubootbaus*, Bernard & Graefe Verlag, Koblenz 1986. (This excellent two-volume work supercedes the original edition, which has been translated into English as *The U-boat*, Arms and Armour Press, 1981.)

Rössler, Eberhard, *Die deutschen Uboote und ihre Werften*, Bernard & Graefe Verlag, Munich, 1979. (Two very good volumes about German shipbuilding yards.)

Rössler, Eberhard, *Die Torpedoes der deutschen Uboote*, Koehler Verlag, Herford, 1984.

Ruge, F, *Sea Warfare 1939–45*, Cassell, London, 1957

Ruge, F, *In vier Marinen*, Bernard & Graefe Verlag, Munich, 1979. (The author served in the Kriegsmarine and became the first Chief of the Federal German Navy.)

Salewski, Michael, *Die deutsche Seekriegsleitung*, Bernard & Graefe Verlag, Frankfurt, 1970. (Two volumes.)

Showell, Jak P Mallmann, *U-boats under the Swastika*, Ian Allen, Weybridge. First edition 1973, second revised and altered edition with different photographs 1987. Translated as *Uboote gegen England*, Motorbuch Verlag, Stuttgart, 1974.

Showell, Jak P Mallmann, *The German Navy in World War Two*, Arms and Armour Press, London, 1979. Translated as *Das Buch der deutschen Kriegsmarine*, Motorbuch Verlag, Stuttgart, 1980.

Showell, Jak P Mallmann, *Germania International*, The German Navy Study Group, 78 Barnfield Crescent, Telford, Shropshire TF1 2EX, England. (Available only through subscription.)

Sorge, Siegfried, *Der Marineoffizier als Führer und Erzieher*, Mittler & Sohn, Berlin, 1943.

Verband Deutscher Ubootsfahrer, Schaltung Küste, Hamburg. (Journal of the German Submariners Association.)

Vorträge zur Marinegeschichte, Vol 2 – *Menschenführung in der Marine*, Militärgeschichtliches Forschungsamt, E S Mittler & Sohn, Herford, 1981.

Waddington, C H, *OR in WW2*, Paul Elek, London, 1973. (About operational research during the war.)

Wagner, G, *Lagevorträge des Oberbefehlshaber der Kriegsmarine vor Hitler 1939–45*, J F Lehmanns Verlag, Munich, 1972.

Watts, A J, *The U-boat Hunters*, Macdonald and Jane's, London, 1976.

Witthöft, H J, *Lexikon zur deutschen Marinegeschichte*, Koehlers, Herford, 1977. (Two most interesting reference volumes.)

Y'Blood, William T, *Hunter Killer*, US Naval Institute Press, 1983.

The important unpublished sources are listed in the acknowledgements.

Index

U-boats listed in map captions and Dönitz in the main text have not been indexed.

Where the name appears throughout a chapter, only the first page has been indexed.

Page numbers in italic indicate that the reference is in a map or caption.

Index of Personalities

Index of Ships and Boats